TAKE
MY
ADVICE

LETTERS TO THE NEXT GENERATION
FROM PEOPLE WHO KNOW A THING OR TWO

Edited by James L. Harmon

SIMON & SCHUSTER
New York London Toronto Sydney Singapore

SIMON & SCHUSTER
Rockefeller Center
1230 Avenue of the Americas
New York, NY 10020

Book design by Ellen R. Sasahara

Manufactured in the United States of America

1   3   5   7   9   10   8   6   4   2

Library of Congress Cataloging-in-Publication Data is available.

ISBN 0-7432-1092-1

For information regarding special discounts for bulk purchases,
please contact Simon & Schuster Special Sales at
1-800-456-6798 or business@simonandschuster.com

For my mother, Christina Marie Blackburn Harmon

Who said Socrates and Plato were just quoting their mothers?
Christina Harmon on her honeymoon, July 1959.

And for Wayne Koestenbaum

Acknowledgments

This may be the longest acknowledgments page in the history of publishing, but just deal with it.

Very special thanks to the talented Mr. Keithley. Todd, you resurrected these letters from public storage and I'm eternally grateful. The publishing world misses you. To Philip Berman, who opened the first door and whose book, *The Courage of Conviction*, was a major inspiration for *TMA*. Thanks to Matt Walker, the hippest editor in the Universe (with the patience of a saint), and to my agent, Michael Bourret, whose advice I'll always take.

I'm indebted to four people who, with their love, friendship, and support, were always willing to stop and smell neuroses. You made this book possible: Tracy Helene Thomas, truly the smartest, most creative woman on the planet; Roger Rand, whose image, if gracing the jacket of this book, would sell a million copies on his photo alone; Randy Bossert, the brother I've always wanted; and Misti Nelson, my eternal Goddess. I love you.

When Bettie Page gives you advice, you take it—like a man! So I'd like to show my parents that I love them by thanking them for all the good things they've done for me: Thanks to my mother for praying her heart out (a woman who can still fit perfectly into her wedding dress— 42 years married, size 2), and my father for allowing me to mooch off him considerably while finishing this book (you'll get the money back, Dad). Thanks to my sisters, Rebekah, LaNae, and Kim and Howard for putting up with me, but don't even try giving me advice. Love to Christopher, Jacob, Nicole, Danielle, and little Moriah Grace. Krystal Joy, mind your mother (see Veruschka's piece).

And readers, if the following reeks of any name-dropping you can bite me: I'm beholden to Bob Shacochis (young men, advice here: run, don't walk, to your nearest bookstore and buy *Easy in the Islands*—it will change your life!); Bruce Benderson, (ditto *User*); Mary Gaitskill; Mark Dery; Chris Kraus; Stewart Home; Jennifer Belle; and the late Patricia Highsmith, all of whom went beyond the call of duty as contributors. And if you don't know who the writers in this book are, you *should.* My gratitude goes to Stuart J. Murray; Michael Ferguson; Timothy Greenfield-Sanders (and Karen, Toby, and Will); Maurice Vellekoop; Francesco Scavullo and Sean Byrnes; Savas Abadsidis; Bruce Weber; Elizabeth Taylor; David Foster Wallace and Mark Leyner (in the beginning, my own personal Rilkes); David Lynch and Barry Gifford (I tried, guys); Eydie Gorme; Connie Francis; Ann-Margret; Camille Paglia for still coming through with a submission during the most horrific time in American history; Mike Albo; Christopher Hitchens (Master H, you still owe me a paragraph—or dinner, your pick); John Waters and Dennis Dermody; THE INCOMPARABLE ANN MAGNUSON; Gloria Vanderbilt, bell hooks for inspiration; Jack Mitchell; David Leddick; Juliet Hacking from the Beaton Estate and Julia Collins from the Harvard Theatre Collection; and everyone from the Lee Miller Archives; and William Claxton and Peggy Moffitt. Thanks to Jo Stafford, Anita O'Day, Kay Starr, and Ted Nugent who told me the way it is. Thanks to Kaye Ballard and friend for being nice to me on my first day. J. K. Potter; Nancy Stender; Pat Miller; Lillian Evey; Robert Strom; Andrew, the freaky park ranger; Bob Van Riper; Matthew Stadler ("sigh"); James Grauerholz; Wayne Stanley; Phillip Ward; John C. Van Doren; Danielle Von Luhmann of CMG; Michael Merrill and the Bette Davis Foundation; the brilliant Ted Landry; Marsha Bacon; Robert Freedman; Doug Ainge (smart influences); Norma, that cool Italian lady I met outside Trader Joe's; Alysia Ball; Lisa Stone; Jennifer from Oblation; Jay and Todd, that sex God. Jim Goad, Rutger Thiellier, Robert Strom, Michael R. Lee, Gwen Morehead, Ross and Kayreen Arnold, JoAnn and B.L., Judy Thomas, Michael Klein, Kim, Kellia Jenkins, and Terry Manning. For letting me spew over the years, thanks to Vicki, Heather, David and Marcos and Susan "Wonder Woman" Carey. Thanks to my Uncle Clyde and Aunt Barbara, my cousin Kami, Maggie and Phil Sund, the wondrous Darlene, Jamie and Lori from Rite Aid, Nancy Klug, my too groovy Kinko's boy, Danny Seim of the band MENOMENA (somebody sign these guys, pronto!), Sue Goffard (Mario, give that girl a raise!). Murray McDonell; my Uncle Allen; Eric Rauth; Helen Lane; the ravishing Ray Rivera; Etta and Buck Waterfield (Jane Russell Rocks!); Virtic Brown; Yale Wagner; Boyd Babbitt; Fernando Del Bosque; Alex Monreal; Cross De Milo; Chris Hiestand; Sam the man from the Palm Desert Library; Sylvere Lotringer; that highly enlightened stud muffin DAVID TRUJILLO; Lynne Hansen; Neal Peters; David Smith; and that very wise man, Greg Mann. My sexy cookie girl, Erica Garvey; Al Wayne; Ken Lease; Nancy Basil; Gail and Larry Denis; Jean Sweitzer; Mary Lea; the luscious Kirsten Jenkins (I got chills, they're multiplyin'); Jessie Dawes; Alicia Joy; Dawn Burnham and Ronnie Balog; Jeff Maul and "Bobbie-licious" Howe and Trevor; Yvette Lucero (where the hell are you?). LeeAnn and John Earlenbaugh (and Stephanie, Dana, and Janna); and Theresa; Heidi; and Virginia. Thanks to Scott Mills, Dick Albertson and Wayne Kulie, Joseph Schooley, Paul and Kathleen Gillmouth and family, and my favorite Jewish Princess, Jeanie Breall. I can't mention everyone, but thanks to all of my friends and family from Scari's: Lou Hijar, Diane Dewald, Susan Fee, Jan and Nick, Sharon Ebel, Faye Contras, Mel, Scott, Greg Holm (when he's acting normal) and Stacey, that sexpot Tina Abney, Andi Park, MARGEE!, Maggie, Dawn, Karen, Tracey, Karri, Lori, and Anita and Pearl—I dig you girls. Special thanks to John and Jo, Connie, Ruth and Larry, and Don and Dottie Markman. And to all of the waiters and waitresses marrying their ketchups from Portland to Paraguay, this one's for you. I'd like to thank all of my one-night stands and every librarian in the tri-county area, with the exception of the two Evil Queens at a certain provincial branch (you know who you are). Special thanks to Denise Holmes; Colleen Winters; Kiera Koester; Robyn Cram; Dana Gale; Cindy Stanley; E'Raina Hatch; and in loving memory, Jane Babcock. Thanks to my voluptuous espresso girl, Ramona Odierna at Café Dolce. Love and appreciation to Andrew Hodgdon, Nan Travers, and little Bella—you handled my meltdowns quite well over the years (they were justified and you know why). Thanks to Charlie Huffman for the laughs and tears (see Joe Dallesandro's piece, baby) and Mark Gillmouth for the laughs and tears (see Joe Dallesandro's piece, baby). Sadie, Max, Bruno-Ricardo, Daisy and Peaches for the love and kisses.

My appreciation extends to all of the publicists, agents, and assistants who allowed me to drive them over the edge.

I'd like to thank the following people, all of whom inspired a young editor: Mr. Gottlieb, Mr. Korda, Ms. Graham, Ms. Snow, Mr. Cerf, Tina Brown needs to give me a job, Mr. Warhol, Mr. Brodovitch, and Diana "You don't have to be born beautiful to be wildly attractive" Vreeland.

I LOVE OPRAH I LOVE OPRAH I LOVE OPRAH I LOVE OPRAH I LOVE OPRAH

A note to critics and reviewers: This is the first book I've edited and I'm currently taking night classes at the Maureen Dowd School of Backbiting, so don't *even* fuck with me. (And the first ignoramus to use the already tired phrase, "Take *My* Advice, *James*," will be deemed a cretin by me, personally, publicly, on the telly, *live.*)

A special thank you to my guardian angels, Mr. Joe Williams, Ms. Ella Mae Morse, and Ms. Carmen McRae. In my darkest moments you always hit me smack dab in the middle with loads of love.

And finally, for taking part in my epistolary madness, I'm indebted to the hundreds, perhaps thousands, of talented people who took the time to compose these exquisite letters. Due to length and legal restrictions, I was unable to include everyone in this volume (from Menninger to Lessing, Vidal to Murdoch). My hope, someday, is to publish a complete, unedited version. Please note that I thank each and every one of you from the bottom of my heart. This is your book.

Contents

"Un jeune homme ne doit pas acheter de valeurs sûres."

—Jean Cocteau

"I learned an awful lot in Little Rock, and here's some advice I'd like to share . . ."

—Marilyn Monroe in
Gentlemen Prefer Blondes

Introduction

"You'll take it and like it."

—HUMPHREY BOGART, from *The Maltese Falcon*

"All artists are two-headed calves."

—TRUMAN CAPOTE, from *Conversations with Capote*

Boy, did I ask for it.

It's not easy being an anachronism. What kind of freak in this day and age would sit down and solicit letters of advice? Well, I'm that freak—and I've got a lot of explaining to do.

Take My Advice, the collection you are now holding, was intended to be published over a decade ago. I'm a lucky person, in that if I walk into a bookstore, my nose will lead me to the exact book I should read at the time. When I was twenty-one, that book was Rainer Maria Rilke's *Letters to a Young Poet*. For those burgeoning young adults unfamiliar with it, the book is a collection of ten silver-tongued letters written between 1902 and 1908 from the poet Rilke to Franz Kappus, who, like me, was a young, struggling artist seeking a bit of guidance in his world. Rilke was a truly sagacious cat—and only twenty-seven at the time—and he touched upon all of the concerns that were swirling through my head: love, doubt, fear, sex, and, especially, art.

While his words of counsel are timeless and the book pretty much became my bible, I was living in a different time. Nowadays, being an ultra-sensitive creature is more of an embarrassing curse than a blessing. What would Rilke say, in those years leading up to the twenty-first century, to an angry, cynical, ironic, black-clad, café-dwelling, cigarette-puffing, wannabe-artist poseur like me? I wanted to find out. And perhaps a contemporary version of the book could be of help to those kindred spirits of mine—a book that would act as a direct line to those dilettantes hoping to segue into being serious artists, those outcasts, misfits, and black sheep.

To his successors I posed a genuinely sincere question: "If you could offer the young people of today one piece of advice, what would it be?" And while my query did open up a veritable can of worms—the pros and cons of simply asking for and taking advice—the response was overwhelmingly positive. I sold the idea in good faith to a publisher that it would be a fresh, illuminating collection of letters to the young artist just starting out. Then all hell broke loose.

I realized very early on the publisher and I did not share the same vision. I was sent list after list of so-called notables to include, and I couldn't stomach it. We're talking grade-B television stars, motivational speakers, phony politicians, cheesy talk-show hosts, and the like. You get the picture. I had to avoid Kathie Lee at all cost! And on the horizon, a toxic cloud of tepid-broth wisdom was mushrooming out of a certain series of books, blanketing chain stores the world over. In my small way, I wanted to combat this. What the publisher wanted was a warm, gooey book with the shelf life of a banana, the literary equivalent to "Up with People." And while *Take My Advice* might never reach the soupy sales of those books, I was damn sure it was going to be different. Being a discerning and critical-minded creature by nature, I ignored what I was told (a bit contradictory when compiling a book on taking advice) and went ahead soliciting those I truly did admire, most of them controversial: outspoken provocateurs, funky philosophers, cunning cultural critics, social gadflies, cyberpunks, raconteurs, radical academics, literary outlaws, and obscure but wildly talented poets. I then encountered what to me was beyond belief: censorship on the part of my publisher. Eventually, I went through three frustrated editors before finally pulling the book in a fit of exasperation. *Take My Advice* was going to be published my way or not at all (I'm a stubborn Aquarius). I threw the letters into public storage and threw myself into my twenties and didn't look back.

Yet the perspicacity of those missives had seared into my brain. Looking back, I took some of the advice to heart, ignored a lot of it, and learned a lot from the bitch goddess called "experience." Anyone who survives their twenties—and I'm talking surviving well-meaning yet strung-out friends, menial and meaningless manual labor, roommates who are master thieves, *unsolicited* advice from parents on answering machines (skip), and lovers who repeatedly rip out your heart and stomp on it—will realize the insight in Sartre's observation that "Hell is other people." Growing up a child of the '80s and '90s, I'd been accused of being too sneeringly negative, even misanthropic. I've just been blessed with a sharp bullshit detector.

When I hit the big 3-o, I realized I'd never attack any of my other creative endeavors if I allowed these letters to remain unpublished. Hundreds upon hundreds of talented people had sat down to put thought to paper with the hope of lifting the spirits of one despondent youth—and perhaps others. I would be a complete ingrate not to share those thoughts.

I had the amazing luck of finding a new, progressive publisher with vision, one who understood exactly what I was going for. I also began writing people whom I felt might have something timely and original to say as we embarked on a new century. And this time I was more direct in my inquiry (just because you're over thirty doesn't mean you have all of the answers). As a young thirtynothing now, I wanted to pick the brains of those people I felt had truly seen it, done it, been there, and survived. These are people over thirty you *can* trust: Left over from my distracted twenties, my Dionysian traits were still outweighing the Apollonian (get Paglia!), my own feelings of shallowness (see Mark Simpson), my craving for the material (Lydia Lunch's "Consumer Revolt"), the gravitational pull I feel toward beauty ("If You Have to Be Beautiful" by Joe Dallesandro), and being a total loser amorously, I wanted a really smart chick to write on the subject of love (check out Judith Butler's "Doubting Love").

I now realize that when I began writing these letters, what I really wanted was assurance that I wasn't alone in the way I felt about the world and where we were headed. And, to be sure, this anthology would never have reached completion if not for the fact that I am a complete, hundred-percent freaky-boy obsessive. Chris Kraus's marvelous letter gave me solace.

The final piece of advice herein comes from the first artist who answered my query, actress Katharine Hepburn. She's nearing ninety-five. She mentions spirit. If you are young and starting out and are dreaming of becoming an artist of any sort, people will do their best to squelch, choke, and just plain break your spirit. Why people do this, I don't know. Now that I'm old enough, I feel it's appropriate to offer my own little bit of advice here: Believe in the gifts you've been given in this life and fight anyone to the death who attempts to douse that spirit.

And the only advice I take anymore? In the end, I still find myself going back to my dog-eared copy of Rilke: "Don't search for the answers. The point is to live everything. Live your questions now. Perhaps, then, someday far in the future, you will gradually, without even noticing it, live your way into the answers."

Bob Shacochis
Writer

Surviving Bad Advice

I can't pretend otherwise—as an advice-taker, I've been as deaf as a
fence post: I have a terrible record. Terrible. I mean, *rotten!* Don't tell
me how to swing a golf club, study for an exam, write a story, make a
living; don't advise me not to smoke cigarettes, and whatever you do,
don't suggest ways I can be a better person. I don't want to hear it.
I'm stubborn and mule-headed and independent to a fault, sure, but
the truth is, I've never been able to stomach advice-givers. It's not
that I never wanted advice, not that I never sought guidance or
yearned for some slice of illumination to help me out of a dark
place—sometimes violently, sometimes as quiet as an infiltrator.

It's just that advice, the readily available and eternally stale sup-
ply of it, always seemed to me to be so poorly packaged—wrapped in
transparent dogma (as when it came from religious institutions), or
fastidiously ribboned in the bias of the status quo (as when it came
from the government), lumped in burlap sacks of authoritarianism
or measured out into silk pouches of righteousness (from church or
government again, or from parents, teachers, cops, bankers, older
brothers, younger sisters, the people next door, athletes and coaches,
movie stars, Ann Landers, anybody and everybody). Whenever I heard
someone growl, *I'm going to show the bastards,* I understood that the
bastards were likely to be advice-givers.

Advice has always been a seller's market—you could get into the
business without a license, and there were no rules and regulations
to hold you back; if you wanted to, you could call shit orange sherbet
and peddle it for five bucks a scoop. So . . . I confess to feeling, at the
very least, a bit uneasy about whomever was buying. Were they fools,
were they desperate, didn't they have enough sense to figure things
out for themselves? Well, too bad for them then. They'd listen to any
voice, however fraudulent; their hopes would be seduced by any

crackpot solution or capricious idea; they'd be soothed by any plat-
itude. Because, too often, advisors grew rich in a monopoly of
absolutes. For me, though, these absolutes were nothing more than
a stockpile of poisons.

Blasphemy is owning God, owning reality, never being wrong.

I can tell you this: Growing up, I never heard one good, solid,
honest, creative, stimulating, life-affirming piece of advice from
the people who happened to be doling it out. What I heard instead
was a chorus of voices singing Back Off, Back Off, don't go near the
edge, shorten thy horizons, be content with letting your heart grow
fat and easy. For me, *not* taking advice became a matter of survival.
Trying to survive my own willfulness until I could build a context of
experience to support my own perspective.

Hey, it took a long time; as often as not I felt I was wrong,
deluded, crazy to have dreams and cursed to have ambition. But the
choice was always clear: to allow myself to be coerced by an authority based on power and money and orthodoxy, or to chase after an
elusive authority that derived from excellence and high spirit and
imagination, come what may. Come failure, come disaster, if that's
where it took me.

Along the way, someone told me something. A small thing,
really, but it stuck, it became important, in a manner I wasn't even
aware of until recently, when I was living in Rome.

During college in the early '70s, I would come home to the East
Coast on summer breaks and work construction. The first summer I
hired on as a laborer; the second summer I had learned enough to
be a carpenter's helper. I worked with a crew from Luray, Virginia,
up in the mountains. They would leave Luray at 4:00 in the morning
and caravan into the suburbs of Washington, D.C., where the job site
was. They were a rough bunch, unrepentant half-literate cracker-
balls, and I was a longhaired dope-smoking antiwar activist college
student. Each Monday they would merrily recount their grand
patriotic adventures of the weekend—ambushing unwary hippies up
in the mountains, punching their lights out, shaving their heads. I

thought these fellows were all tease and bluster, until one of them was arrested for assault on a pair of campers, a young man and a woman. Anyway, their worldview was, let's say, *limited*, and the only thing I felt I shared with men of a caliber this low was the ice water from the Igloo cooler.

I was assigned to work with the leader of the crew, the head carpenter, a hugely muscled hillbilly with brilliantined hair and Elvis sideburns, who took gruff pleasure in tolerating a boy like me. He liked to brag about drinking moonshine until he was blind, wrestling black bears in the woods, and beating up queers. He worked me hard, he worked my backside off, without mercy but not without fairness, because he worked as if he were the devil on deadline. And he was, despite his raw unforgiving style as a man, a master of his craft, and in this way absolutely worthy of respect. He was stunningly fluent in the language of tools and materials, had a genius for the meticulous logic of structure and building, and, above all—and in spite of his distaste for my values—he was a natural-born teacher, couldn't help himself and perhaps even knew this was the best thing in him, the best and most enduring part of his character, and he educated his helpers with grace and tenderness and intelligence—virtues in contradiction to the life he shaped for himself off the job.

One day, inspecting a wall I had framed, he set his square to it and, seeing that the lines and angles were not true, he unholstered his hammer and called me over.

"Honey," he said (he called all the helpers *Honey*, that strange endearment between males in the blue-collar south), "it's off, but it ain't so off we couldn't stand her up and nail it. But the little that's wrong with it will just keep right on, growing through the house, unless someone takes care of it or unless it grows so big ain't no one can fix it."

This was a gentle-voiced lecture, but I had no appreciation for it. *Yeah, yeah*, I said to myself, *can the crap*. I did it wrong. I wasn't going to get away with it. I'd have to do it over. Fine.

"No one would know, darlin'," he said, wielding the hammer

in his massive fist, "because the house still going to look like a house when we all through." The hammer kissed first one joint, then another, then he really put all the power of his forearm and wrist into it on opposite corners. He laid his framing square back on the wall and it was perfect.

"Now looky there," he said, winking, which he liked to do. "How many times I have to tell you college boys, when it comes to *making* mistakes, a bad carpenter and a good carpenter is the same. The only difference is, the good carpenter figures out how to correct his."

It was harmless, commonsense, matter-of-fact truth he had delivered, hardly worth mentioning, requiring no thought, almost too obvious to swallow dry. I nodded my head, said "Okay, boss," and went back to work. I learned what I could, the simple tricks of the trade, went back to school, returned the following summer to be hired on at another project as a full-fledged carpenter, but I knew I wasn't all that good at it and so couldn't be happy, and the summer after that I gave it all up and painted houses instead.

The reason I was no good at it wasn't a mystery to me: I just couldn't develop the belief or understand the principle that the mistakes I was making—cutting a board a quarter inch too short, standing up a wall that was a few degrees off plumb—were any big deal, so I never bothered to correct them. Everybody makes mistakes, right? The answer to that is, yes and no.

Eighteen years later, I found myself atop a tower of scaffolding at the Vatican, a privileged visitor to the restoration of the Sistine Chapel, running my fingers across the surface of Michelangelo's masterwork. From the crowded floor of the chapel, looking up, the vault of the ceiling is a seamless universe of exquisite order, interlocking galaxies of exuberant Renaissance colors blocked into distant images and icons, a visual narrative of Creation staggering in its vast symmetry. Taking it all in, its arduous and superhuman enormity, anybody with any sense is humbled to the scale of a flea: The name of Michelangelo takes on the proportions of a *giant*, becomes as meaningful (or meaningless) as saying Exxon, or General Motors, or Sony.

Yes! But ride the rickety workmen's elevator up three stories, watching *The Last Judgment* slide by, to the summit of the scaffolding where the restorers work with their computers and paint jars and ammonia-soaked cotton swabs, and the grandness of the Sistine Chapel becomes breathtakingly intimate—and a miracle of sorts happens: The work of the artist recedes and Michelangelo himself comes tantalizingly into view.

The platform at the top of the scaffolding was cantilevered, corresponding with the arch of the ceiling; its lowest levels were so snug you could lie on your back (as you-know-who did, for three years) and reach out to lightly touch (caress would be more accurate) individual panels of the paintings. And so this is what I did, marveling at the unexpected sensuality of each face, irresistible, the languid pleasure of the expressions, impossible to see from below. As I looked, I began to see the profiles of certain figures in transition. Some had been moved, changed. The scoring in the fresco where the artist had traced the original cartoon, or sketch, of his subject, providing the bold outline of a character—in some places it had been corrected, so that the scoring and the final image were mismatched. Here was a phantom arm, outstretched; there, the realized arm, the arm visitors see from below, had been tucked against the body. Here, the specter of a head turned away from its companion; there, it did not shy from the companion's gaze.

Why was I stunned, why so profoundly impressed? I was looking at Michelangelo's mistakes. Once the wet fresco had hardened, almost five centuries ago, it had preserved its own scrupulous history of the artist's errors and lapses and rethinkings. Michelangelo's mistakes! They were a door into impenetrable genius, and beyond that threshold I was dumbfounded to encounter, after so long a time, the carpenter from Luray. How ridiculous, I thought. What sort of false knowledge could bind an ignorant redneck and a sensibility on the scale of Michelangelo's? But there it was, and the axioms I had assumed were implied by the carpenter's somewhat banal words of wisdom to me were undermined.

Aren't these fallacies: *Everybody makes mistakes* and *People learn from their mistakes*? Isn't it more true that very few people make mistakes, if we define mistakes as *that which must be corrected*? And where is the conclusive body of evidence that people learn from their mistakes? In fact, I don't even think *learning from mistakes* is the right focus to begin with, since it infers there is such a thing as a path to infallibility, which is both a simple-minded and dangerous notion.

Michelangelo's mistakes, frozen within testimony of concrete— what they suggest is that mistakes are, first and foremost, a by-product of the pursuit of excellence. (I'm not talking about criminal acts here—that's another realm that can't be addressed by the euphemism "mistake.") The arena of no-mistakes is not perfectionism, though every pious figure of authority on earth would have you believe this, but mediocrity, complacency—the attitude that I permitted myself as a carpenter, knowing full well what it took to get it right.

Correcting the mistakes, however—that's a different story. It means that, from the floor of the Sistine Chapel, man is divine, but up on the scaffolding, all is the glorious, earnest mess you should expect it to be.

It's the only way to have a soul, isn't it, this patching up, this painting over, this trimming out, this loyalty to compensation?

Dr. John Money
Sexologist

Virtuoso Hand Practice

Today I offer my advice while wearing my academic gown as a doctor of Sexology. Sexology, the science of sex, is a little more than a century old. Its philosophical parent, sexosophy, counts its years not in centuries, but millennia, for sexosophy is as old as religion. Sexosophy is the set of sexual values, beliefs, and principles that, in most societies, is part of its religion.

One of the most ancient of all sexosophical principles is the principle of semen conservation. According to this principle, semen is the most precious of the vital fluids, and its depletion induces degeneracy, disease, and death. Since only males have semen, a derivative of semen-conservation theory is the theory of the innate inferiority and weakness of females. Both theories are incontrovertibly wrong.

In European and American medicine after the 1750s, semen-conservation theory underwent a great revival, replacing demon-possession theory. Males were advised that semen should only be used to create a pregnancy. Terrifying warnings of the consequences of masturbation were issued to the young. These were based on the totally erroneous assumption that the "social disease" now know as the twin scourges of syphilis and gonorrhea was not caused by infection, but by the loss of semen. Germ theory, which would explain their true cause, would not be discovered until the 1870s.

Masturbation, it was said, was caused by lascivious thought and concupiscence of the mind, which in today's language means erotic fantasy. Children's minds were declared to be innocent and pure, and would remain so, even in adolescence, unless they were stimulated by impure thoughts. Pornography was dreaded like the plague, for it was believed to stimulate loss of semen, especially by causing masturbation, and thus in turn sexual disease, degeneracy, and death. The false logic in this reasoning must be one of the greatest intellectual blunders in human history. With the advent of germ theory, it became perfectly obvious that the pleasure of self-stimulation through masturbation actually protects against catching syphilis or gonorrhea.

Masturbation in Latin means, literally, hand rape. *Hand practice,* the term used in India, sounds better. Hand practice, today, is just about the only surefire guarantee against catching the human immunodeficiency virus (HIV), which causes AIDS. I strongly recommend hand practice, especially to youths who are entering adolescence, but also to people of any age who want, at all costs, not to expose themselves inadvertently to the infected body fluids of anyone who is already, even though invisibly, carrying the virus.

Masturbation accompanied by masturbation fantasy is a rehearsal for a sexual relationship with a partner. Masturbation fantasies have been around for as long as the human race has been on earth. Only in the twentieth century, however, have filmmakers in the entertainment industry converted the mental tapes of their own and other people's fantasies into erotically explicit movies and videos, and produced them commercially so that others may share them.

You will not be able to share someone else's erotic fantasy, however, unless it matches your own. People with healthy or normophilic erotic fantasies do not get turned on sexually by books, films, or videos made for people with unhealthy or paraphilic (kinky) erotic fantasies, and they do not catch a paraphilia by reading or watching an example of paraphilic kinkiness.

My recommendation to young people is to select technically superior, erotically healthy videos, and to use them to become champions of virtuoso hand practice. To begin with, you can watch them with your lover, engaging in mutual hand practice but still avoiding contact with each other's body fluids. In that way you will buy time to discover how well matched you are for a long-term, pair-bonded love affair, and maybe even marriage. Eventually the day will arrive when you can make a solemn contract of pair-bonded fidelity, which means that as long as you stay together, neither one will risk infecting the other by breaking the contract and bringing back someone else's AIDS virus.

My final recommendation is that all young people educate all people of the older generation to be rationally open-minded, and to accept my advice. Otherwise the older people will be condemning their children and grandchildren to becoming, in the prime of their lives, very ugly corpses, loved to death by a virus.

Cindy Sherman
Artist

Whether you go to college or get a job, after *finishing* high school, MOVE OUT of your PARENTS' HOUSE.

Learn to be as independent as possible (especially before commiting yourself to anyone or anything).

Develop an interest in learning just for its own sake—choose exactly what matters to you and pursue it. (Using this to creative ends, once you know everything about a subject/technique, etc., you must forget it all and rely on your instincts.)

Richard Meltzer
Music critic, novelist

Very Deep Shit!

The writer as a loaded pistol: The young sex god, Richard Meltzer.

Well first of all, let's get clear on one thing: There are no "generations." Maybe once, but no longer. Or, if you'd like, there is only one. We're all in the shit together. Period.

To cut to the chase, American Youth has never had fewer advantages, assets, resources—not in all the time I've been around, and that includes the loathsome, despicable *pre*-rock fifties (when they banned comic books, and the *best* you could look forward to was wearing a tie every day of your life). Aside from the extra years you've got remaining, your lot is basic NOTHING. Youth is a dismal freaking joke today: a consumer-demographic blip *defined* as maimed and retarded.

Quickly, you're gonna need to think for yourself or (perish!) come up with your own system (no cheating!): It's fucking compulsory.

And then, the long run. Though miracles do happen, it will in all likelihood take you much longer than you expect—an unfair percentage of the time you've got left—to get much of anything right, to develop your own "chops," to arm yourself the way nurturing parents hypothetically once did while you were still in diapers. You have to factor in the LONG HAUL. (Writing, for inst—something I personally wouldn't wish on a dog—will take you *fifteen years*, minimum, to even begin to get right.)

In the meantime, an early order of biz: Unplug from the cyber lifeline—it's a fucking *deathline:* the bitter END of mammal life as any of us have ever known it. And encourage—by hook, crook, or outright subterfuge—everybody ELSE to unplug, y'hear?

And the next order, well, choice of poison. There's no getting very deep into this here life without the faithful assistance of what-sems that at least *partially* will also be killing you. For symptomatic relief, artificial energy, access to alternate universes, superficial kicks, whatever . . . there's no getting around 'em. Still, it would be cheesy to impose my actual tastes on you—like you should drink, let's say, a lot of strong bitter ale . . . avoid red wine until a doctor orders it . . . whiskey will slow you down, put you to sleep . . . if you're young enough, speed probably isn't such a bad idea. Heroin and opiates, on the other hand, really aren't for kicks—they're for *heavy* grief reduction.

Speaking of which, from experience, I would say there's really only one viable program of low-to-mid grief reduction (don't laugh): the blues. Equip yourself—listen to everybody from Charlie Patton to Son House to Memphis Minnie to Robert Wilkins to Robert Johnson to Elmore James and Muddy Waters, Lightin' Hopkins, John Lee Hooker (pre-1960), Howlin' Wolf, Little Walter . . . all the way up to like Otis Rush, Albert Collins, and, okay, Jimi Hendrix. (No Robert Cray.) (And no Stevie Ray Vaughn.) At its best, and I'm not talkin' semi-best, rock as a means to that desired end is a semi-reprise of the blues (never the full dose).

Buddhism? I wouldn't know. Some Beats swore by it, but I've never tried it.

Speaking of Beatniks, don't read *On the Road*, not ahead of four or five other Kerouac titles: *Big Sur, The Subterraneans, Tristessa, The Dharma Bums,* and this one you never heard of called *Vanity of Duluoz.*

Otherwise, I dunno, see the movie *Mesa of Lost Women*—don't ask me why. (I'm sure it's rentable.)

That's it, so anyway, again: 'tain't no generations. Any more than there are "decades." But some *very* deep shit. Get used to it.

Mary McCarthy
Writer, critic

Be truthful, within the limits of possibility, and pay attention. I would also recommend the avoidance of credit cards.

The eyes of Mary McCarthy.
Senior portrait, 1933.
Photo by Chidnoff

Robert Creeley
Poet

What seems most significant is the way in which one takes the world as existing, and much of that comes from the fact of one's birth and the people of that time and place. One can change the effects of that willfully, but it is often hard even to get rid of them. But I do believe, very much, what the poet Charles Olson told me Herman Melville had as a motto over the table on which he wrote:

Be true to the dreams of thy youth.

No matter the idealism of either Melville's or my own insistence, it would seem nonetheless that the time in one's life when the imagination of possibilities is most articulate, and the sense of their enclosure least restricting, is one's youth. That fact is to be respected, even cared for. It's not very much different than another poet's advice:

Give it your best shot.

Ted Berrigan would also add, "I'd like to take the whole trip." And that he did.

Whatever sense of life one has, it seems to me qualified by the literal biological *thing* we are, and by the fact that, though we may presume differences between us, we're basically, like chickens, not a wildly various life form. Our repetitions are bleakly notorious in every sense. But a world is, it turns out, in the very word that says it, a *"vir* (man)*-eld* (age)," the length of a human life—and what one takes that as being, and what relations one feels it to have or works to accomplish: That's it entirely. If there is a world of insistent pain and poverty and despair, it is a human one. That I have never been able to forget.

Still, feelings seem to me the final human experience and resource, and humor most specifically is our abiding relief. Thank God we can laugh! If I remember anything of final value, it would have to be laughter and love—and the people of one's heart.

Advice may well be another matter. Years ago I was trying to chop wood on a small farm we'd moved to in New Hampshire, and our one real claim on country ways was having got there. The rest was an expectable blank. Our neighbor watched me whack away at the log I was trying to cut through, and said, finally, "Why don't you let the axe do some of the work? If you can lift it, it can fall." He also showed me how to let a crosscut saw ride on its own weight, rather than be pushed and pulled, back and forth, as I was using it. Whatever the scale or application, not much more than that ever gets to be the point.

Robert Creeley

Valerie Martin
Writer

I think it is important to realize that all the solutions our society offers us for the feelings of guilt and powerlessness any thinking person must experience in the face of what society has, in reality, to offer (especially to future generations) are false solutions. Television and radio are particularly reprehensible purveyors of solutions that will only make things worse. The despair that causes the individual to prefer mindless noise to silence is the most dangerous of all and results in a deadening of all proper sensibility, all sensibility to one's fellows and one's position in the natural scheme of things, all productive thought, all possibility of clarity and peace. In the grocery store, in our cars, in our living rooms, waiting on the telephone, everywhere we go, we are fed a steady stream of mind-deadening sound, of bad advice, confused ideology, and the constant admonition to be happy.

My advice is simple. When possible, turn off the sound. Don't be overly concerned about being happy. Try to need less, to find work that doesn't demean you. Read more, talk less. Try to raise your own children without television. When despair sets in, as it will, sit quietly and wait it out in silence.

Howard Zinn
Historian

Advice to the young:
> Read Peter Kropotkin's *An Appeal to the Young*.
>
> Read Tolstoy's *The Death of Ivan Ilych*.
>
> Read James Joyce's *The Portrait of the Artist as a Young Man*.

As for my own advice:
Look for independent sources of information beyond the official pronouncements, the mass media, the formal educational system. Go to the library. Understand that money and weapons are fragile forms of power, that human beings, when united in a cause, can make money worthless and weapons futile, that powerless people can create power by unity, sacrifice, risk, commitment. Do not think that nonviolence can bring about a change if it remains passive; it must be linked to direct action. Assume that all governments lie. Do not accept the idea that the violence of war can be justified by claiming to prevent a larger violence. Understand that all war is a war against children, and therefore cannot be justified, whatever the reason. Do not hesitate to speak your mind, even if you are alone in a threatening crowd—you may find surprising allies among those who are too timid to speak out. Listen carefully to the arguments of your opponents, and search for the core of truth in their errors, so you can separate it from what is dangerous. Remember that involvement with other people in the cause of peace and justice is in itself worth doing, whether you "win" or not, because there is victory in every moment of united struggle. Do not give up on anyone. People are infinitely changeable. Live in such a way that your children and grandchildren will be proud of you.

Paul Krassner
Writer, activist

Watch yourself. Watch yourself at all times. Watch yourself as though you were observing a Martian. Watch others as though they were also Martians under observation.

Remember what Krishnamurti said when a disciple asked him, "Why is there evil in the world?" He replied, "To thicken the plot." It's a good theatrical metaphor to filter reality through. Just watch yourself and enjoy the way everybody plays themselves to the hilt all the time.

Try to do nothing for money that you wouldn't do for free. Try to take nothing for free that you wouldn't pay money for. Try to get your money back if the advice in this book doesn't work for you. Try to be honest with yourself for twenty-four hours.

Pretend you're God, but try to be subtle about it. Pretend that everyone else is God and you're not. Pretend you're not making choices every moment—unless you choose to pretend.

Don't take yourself as seriously as your causes. Don't take anything personally. Don't take anything for granted. Don't feel superior to your inferiors. Don't feel inferior to your superiors. Don't litter. Don't blame me.

Only shoplift at the stores that you shop at. Only plagiarize from unknowns. Only remember to breathe, and everything else will fall into place.

Count your blessings. Count your change. Count your changes. Always put the shower curtain inside the bathtub when you take a shower. Always know your endorser. Always cross at the green. Always remember that everybody's perception is their reality. Never get two high colonics on the same day. Never make a separation between selfishness and altruism. Never vomit and laugh simultaneously. Never attempt to recall your social security number in the middle of an orgasm.

Lydia Lunch
Confrontationist, artist

Consumer Revolt

Even for the most politically apathetic, staging your own personal consumer revolt suggests a sneaky and satisfying way to upset the imbalance of financial distribution. Thirty-four percent of the United States of America is living below the poverty line. This has everything to do with nepotism, favoritism, the lack of decent education, prejudice, and this country's incredible ability to turn a blind eye toward

Don't forget your lunch:
The legendary Ms. Lydia.
Photo © J. K. Potter

its own evil, utilizing deception as witnessed most blatantly in the presidential election of 2000, where a privileged "favored son" was instated into the highest seat of power in the free world before even all the votes were counted. His partner, the "vice" president, pulled in thirty-six million dollars in the year preceding the election. If that alone doesn't spark off a revolt, and it hasn't yet, we are truly in sad shape as a nation. Don't help make the rich richer!

Some suggestions to keep the money out of the mega-conglomerates' pockets while spreading your hard-earned and excessively taxed cash dollars into the hands that really work for a living.

1. Avoid all labels. Don't allow yourself to play corporate whore by acting as a walking billboard for huge corporations like Nike, Levi's, Liz Claiborne, Tommy Hillfiger, etc., most of whom have been accused of (yet never tried or convicted for) hiring overseas slave laborers, usually underage and underpaid, to make the clothes they charge you a ridiculous markup to sport so you can play walking advertisement for their devious practices.

2. Avoid anything that says "Made in China." The draconian conditions China still imposes on its billions of human beings means the workers are not profiting (they rarely do) either financially or in terms of basic human rights. Do not sponsor a country that as a rule abuses most of its populace. That means avoiding wholesale slave traders like Target, K-Mart, etc., who buy in bulk and are equally guilty of suspect tactics.

3. Instead, shop locally. Support small businesses and non-chain stores whose labels say "Made in the USA." There are far too many practices to mention here that the United States endorses and I do not, but at least most of the sweatshops have been shut down, and although the minimum wage in this country IS STILL NOT A LIVING WAGE, you can at least be 95 percent certain that a twelve-year-old making fifteen cents an hour is not manufacturing your designer clothes.

4. Recycle your clothes. Trade with friends. When you outgrow them or grow out of them, donate them. Shop at thrift stores, flea markets, swap meets. Much more fun, and definitely puts the cash, or profit, into the private sector. Many thrift shops like the Salvation Army, Veterans of America, and Goodwill donate at least a small percentage of their profits to the needy.

5. Buy food from farmer's markets, small mom-and-pop grocery stores, or food collectives. Anything to avoid the conglomerate food-mongers making more cash by supporting the corporate pig and cattle farmers, who have wiped out small farms, desecrated the land, continued to pollute, and are now self-regulating themselves since the Food and Drug Administration no longer polices their often criminally negligent safety standards.

6. Avoid McDonalds, Burger King, Wendy's, etc. Not only do you NOT KNOW exactly what goes into their "beef burgers," but the billions of dollars they have made never trickle down into the hands of the workers manning the tills. Their marketing tactics, aimed mostly at children, are helping turn us into a country of junk-food junkies whose high cholesterol count is a heart attack waiting to happen. Respect your body and in the long run it will respect you. Abuse it with garbage, and it will eventually revolt against you.

7. Don't drive. Or drive less and carpool. Be revolutionary and buy an electric car. Seventy miles to the gallon! Why put hard-earned cash into the hands of greedy monopolists whose sole goal is to rape the planet and rob her of her bodily fluids? Bike. Scooter. Public transport. All reasonable alternatives.

8. Don't use credit cards. Or use them only if you're sure you can pay them off within a six-month period. I understand the temptation. If the whole world is in debt, why shouldn't I be? There's no better way to self-strangulate than by running up bills you not only can't pay off, but will be paying interest on for years to come.

9. Shop very carefully if you're considering student loans. If you go into default and your account is turned over to a collection agency, you will be paying outrageous fees and interest, usually higher than on most major credit cards. They can also be spiteful enough to go in and garnish any future paychecks you might earn. Be very, very cautious.

I know people in their forties who are still paying for classes they attended in their twenties, which led neither to profit nor intellectual gain. Be very crafty about how much time and money you are willing to invest or waste on a college education.

10. Recycle, trade, and share CDs and books. The profit record companies and publishing companies gain versus the royalties they pay back to artists is ridiculous anyway. Support live shows. Buy merchandise directly from the bands or authors. Investigate their websites. At least the money you spend will go directly into the pocket of the artist.

Staging a mini—consumer revolt is easy. Pay attention to where every single one of your hard-earned dollars is going. After all, only you know exactly what kind of bullshit you had to do in order to earn them in the first place.

Cunning Lingis: Portrait of the young sensualist.

Alphonso Lingis
Philosopher

To Have Been Dangerous

We feel hungers, thirsts, lacks, and wants. We feel our weaknesses, our vulnerability, an inner emptiness. We grasp for content. We work to acquire cash, restaurant meals, designer clothes, a suburban house, a high-definition television, and a Porsche.

The things we acquire are assimilated, annexed to ourselves. Contentment is the pleasure simmering over a content assimilated. It is an inert and torpid state. Possessed by possessions, we are secure about ourselves, like the termites of the African savannah, living entirely inside their high-rise constructions, an environment of their own making.

Schooling teaches us how to succeed, but we do not understand life until we have watched someone being born and someone dying.

Anyone who has done it knows it makes sense, if it is all you can manage, to save up for years in order to take off at least a few days from work and responsibility and fly to France just to see the *Mona Lisa*, fly to Japan just to spend a morning in the Ryoanji Zen sand garden in Kyoto, fly to Peru just to spend a day in Machu Picchu.

There is an inner desolation in every human life that speaks to only human voices and grasps only human hands, caresses only human bodies. Our life is by nature destined to know life, speak with the voices of antelopes and Bactrian camels, gaze into the gaze of owls and octopods, fondle the faces of cats and zebras, skip and soar with robins and albatross, hum and chant with bumblebees and locusts, creep and shimmer with caterpillars and silverfish.

We do not know what is, if we do not know great joys, great pains!

Joy is that surge that breaks out of the compound where possessions accumulate and gratification is oral; it is finding oneself swept away into inhuman spaces. The exhilaration of ocean diving or hang gliding are not simply the satisfaction of "knowing one's mettle," of "proving oneself." One finds oneself existing in the oceanic depths, in the skies. Seventy-five percent of earth's surface is ocean. When you go into the ocean you realize that until then you did not know the planet.

Ecstatic states change the perceptual space-time coordinates, making us enter a universe of microperceptions, molecular kaleidoscopes, scintillations, and irradiations. Swimmers who swim the British Channel set out with that integration of all faculties Saint-Exupery found in night flying. But as they swim, their minds empty out, the mental awareness of the difficulties and the methods to deal with them fades away, the attention to dangers and to the goal itself dissolves in the waves, and they enter into something of the no-mind state achieved by adepts of Zen. The rhythms of the strokes, of the waves, of the sun, of the clouds moving overhead, fill them with their redundance.

When you descend into the ocean, you discover coral reefs richer in things to see, in colors and patterns and forms of life, than any environment on the surfaces. But in the oceanic deep you are only a visitor; this richness does not enrich you. Almost at once you realized how pointless it was to bring a camera down there; the colors of the fish exist in watery movement through the streaks of sunlight, and the most beautiful slides show even less of the fish than the fisherman who has hooked one out and shows it dead under the dry sun. You lose not only the upright posture defining you as a human being, but also the swim strokes you learned to move across the surface. You make yourself buoyant with iron weights and move with rubber fins; you catch on to how the fish steer and ride the surge. You see the fish as fish see—watery streaks and shimmers in the liquid sunlight—but this vision cannot be brought back out of the water. You found that when you were back in the boat and tried to identify the fish you had seen below, the problem was not only that the pictures in the field guide were so inadequate to what the fish moving in the deep looked like, but that you could not remember what forms they had and what designs decorated them. Your surface perception, your terrestrial memory, dissolve when you descend into the briny deep, and your watery movements, visions, and intelligence dry up as soon as you break the surface. Those who go to the sea have so little to say about it, become taciturn, which is sometimes mistaken for profundity, but those who descend into the deep do not bring the depth back in themselves when they surface. You can only know the ocean by returning to it, descending again to become another fish, become oceanic.

You will set off for coral reefs no human eyes have yet seen. You will be moved to rise to the skies. You will head into virgin Alpine forests in Bhutan and rain forests in Borneo. You will long to descend into the rock core of the earth. Going down to the depth of the Grand Canyon where the Shiva schist is only here exposed to the light, going down the tubes bored for the pharaohs in the Valley of the Kings of Luxor. You will not have known ice until you have wandered the summits of the Andes and trekked as high as your lungs can manage in the Himalayas, until you have visited Antarctica, where 70 percent of earth's fresh water is frozen in centuries-old ice.

The ecstasy of going into the ocean, into the skies, into the rock core of the earth, into the ice is a pleasure radically different from the contentment that simmers over possessions. You will be dispossessed of apparatus to capture images and memories, dispossessed of memory and foresight, of your identity, of your human upright posture and bodily skills. You will be adrift in the immensities and sublimities of reality. You will know extreme emotions, great joys and great pains. You will weep the bitterest tears and roar with the wildest laughter, your hands will extend blessings and curses. You will know reality.

People make the mistake of trying to reach the depths and the heights alone. One needs a bearer. It happens that in the night and the long loneliness of the mountains, the desert, or the ice, the torments of your flesh move you to respond to a chance encounter with another oblivion-seeker, outcast in the desert, wanderer in the mountains. Someone without civic and urban identity offers her or his body, abyss of unmarked wounds and dark exhilarations. You abandon yourself to monstrous kisses and caresses. You denude yourself and give yourself over to the strange passions of a stranger; you give yourself over to the risks of strangling, rape, ill-treatment, insults, cries of hatred, unleashing of whole, deadly passions. You lose yourself in bestial and reptilian lusts. "In the middle of the night, in the middle of the bed, between the sheets, an almost wordless language, or one that makes words mean their opposite is forged between two lovers," Jean Genet writes. "Wherever it occurs, this nocturnal language between two lovers creates a night. They take refuge in it even among a thousand or a hundred thousand others, who may have held their noses at the moisture of their reunion."[1] You part without compensation or exaction.

Two practical rules are all you need:

1. Do it right away! Think of the most expansive, exultant experience imaginable. Skiing Antarctica? Skydiving? Rafting down the Amazon? Visiting Angkor Wat or the Galapagos? Go there now! Never be afraid that the world will appear more mediocre by contrast after—you will find new heights and depths in places that before looked closed in their somnolence.

2. Believe your happiness! Never make any important decision out of depression, a sense of needs, of dependency. If you choose to get married because you are feeling lonely, afraid of becoming unattractive as you age, afraid of being uncared for in old age, then you will marry badly. Make every important decision in a state of exultation. Is it on the dance floor that you feel right, your body feels right, you never have to urge yourself to go, you never want to leave? Then decide to be there, to become a dancer, whatever the costs, the uncertainties, the counsels of prudence pressed on you!

An old Palestinian woman said to Jean Genet, "To have been dangerous for a thousandth of a second, to have been handsome for a thousandth of a thousandth of a second, to have been that, or happy or something, and then to rest—what more can one want?"[2]

Notes

1. Jean Genet, *Prisoner of Love*, trans. Barbara Bray (Hanover, NH: University Press of New England), p. 329

2. Ibid., p. 234

Spalding Gray
Performer

The advice that I have for young people today is that they try to get in touch with the fact of their own mortality, in a creative way that is not self-destructive. Most young people have no sense that they are really going to die. I didn't until I was sixteen and rolled the family car. That cured me—but I don't think of it as a creative cure.

I'd advise young people to go visit morgues and see as many dead bodies as they can. The Buddhists used to do that, and maybe still do. They called that stuff the "graveyard meditations."

There's no doubt in my mind that once you begin to have a clear sense that you're going to die, you really begin to live—and that's all there really is, because the meaning of life is in the living of it.

Joe Dallesandro
Actor

If You Have to Be Beautiful

When I was a kid working in the movies, people kept telling me they thought I was beautiful, but I didn't really know what to do with that information. It didn't register. I never thought of myself as a really good-looking man. I'm short. I'm stocky. I don't know where the good looks come in. Honestly. I know beauty when I see it and all I can say is that I've had a few photographs taken of me where I look better than I feel in real life.

The first time I met Henry Fonda, I saw these blue blue blue eyes and I said, man, that's a movie star; that's why he's a movie star. He was an old man when I met him, but there was still that sparkle, that star quality that you felt somewhere inside. And it wasn't because I had seen him in so many movies that I was simply awed by the man's reputation. You would know this person was special even if you had never seen him in the movies. That's the difference. I walk down the street and I'm just the next guy getting on the bus.

Was Henry Fonda known for his beauty? Not in the same

After the flesh: Little Joe, superstar, March 2, 1970.
Photo copyright Jack Mitchell, used with permission

way as Brad Pitt. But all you had to do was take one look at this person to see how he sparkled.

The negative aspect of beauty in our culture is our obsession with it—like when a person becomes bulimic or anorexic because they want to look like a celebrity or a model in a magazine. You don't have to rob a bank to get the money to buy a beautiful car. It's the wrong behavior.

With all the gyms we have, everybody thinks you have to be physically fit or you're a dog. It's wonderful for the person who can be physically fit, but for the person who struggles with it, it's terrible. There shouldn't be such importance put on it. What you look like does not determine what you can be in your life.

Ultimately, I owe my success as an actor to my fans. An actor is in the weird position of basing some level of success on the opinions of people he doesn't know and who really don't know him. You're just an image. In a way, it's how most of us live our lives. We wonder if other people find us worthy, find us smart, find us attractive, find us valuable.

Something we all neglect is that it's not for us to be taking somebody else's inventory. It's not for us to be judging somebody else. The only important person we need to be judging is ourselves— we become stronger and better people when we take stock of who we are. That's important, something we need to do on a regular basis. You may do it in school or college because you're asked to—you have to get so much information for the quiz next week; you have to store up all sorts of information. In some situations you're always taking inventory of how much you know or where you're at—in your studies or in your job situation, but people need to do it in general. Also, pay attention to your relations with others. Ask yourself, *Did I just think about myself today or did I think about others, or how I could be helpful to another person?* We go out of our way to entertain ourselves all the time, but why don't we go out of our way to be helpful or useful to other people? Sure, some of us do it, but we wouldn't have such a need for it if there were more. We have to scream about blood drives because people don't donate blood.

So if you happen to be beautiful—that is, if you happen to be what people think they find attractive—then have fun with it, because it's not going to last. Make the rounds, strut your stuff if it makes you feel important; have some dirty pictures taken to look back on when things get wrinkled—but realize that's all playtime and you've got to have balance to your life.

When you're young, you're given a plate and you're given all sorts of things to choose from, and whoever your guardian is should be trying to give you a balanced meal. They should be saying, You've got to have some vegetables, have some steak, have a little religion, have the school, have this, have that. Not until you get much older do you realize that you need all these things in your life. I had a

> **From my point of view, it made perfect sense to start avoiding the kind of film in which I walked around the room with my pants off while transvestites screamed at me.**

religious upbringing, for instance, and I took note. It wasn't about the religion, a specific faith or doctrine; it was about living a principled life where you don't lie, you don't cheat, you don't steal.

Years later I threw that away, lost control, and got into trouble with alcohol and drugs and all sorts of bad behavior. It was like a contest to see how many things I could steal before I got my head shot off or something. It came close to that before I was scared into being good for a while. It took years for me to understand that I needed to achieve a balance in my life.

In acting, as in life, listening is the key to learning. During my days making movies for Andy Warhol and Paul Morrissey, there was a period when I shut my mouth. I was a well-known nontalker surrounded by all the craziness of the people in the films. For a while I was like that off-screen too. I knew there were a lot of people out there smarter than me, and there was a lot more to learn if my mouth was shut than if it was moving. At a certain age, years later, I stopped doing that and became a person who ran around thinking that I knew it all. I became unteachable. That was the most devastating behavior of my life. It messed up so many things for me, including decisions that I made about my career. From my point of view, it made perfect sense to start avoiding the kind of film in which I walked around the room with my pants off while transvestites screamed at me. The people who'd given me this wonderful opportunity to have a career and travel all over the world never saw me grow. They never saw me as anything but some street person. I felt I had done a lot more than just be an underground film poster boy, but I also felt I was never given any respect where I was looking for it the most. And that kind of pissed me off.

Imagine that: an actor getting pissed off because he's been successfully typecast. I think it was because I didn't have major hang-ups about my body when I was young and was so casual about nudity onscreen that people got caught up looking at the surface. I know what it means to be judged based on appearances. When people met me who knew my work in the Warhol/Morrissey films, most of them assumed that I was the character that I played. I've always said my range is not very big—I play Joe Dallesandro in every film, but with a different name. People who didn't know the films, though, met another person.

An artist is someone who doesn't generally get paid a lot of money. An artist is somebody who eats jelly sandwiches for most of their life. They struggle. They have hard times. If it's what they love, if it gives them pleasure and satisfaction, then they stay with it. Maybe you'll never have success, but maybe you will. Nobody can predict what's going to happen. Even in the acting profession, nobody can decide who's going to be the star beyond one lucky break.

Young actors looking for advice about breaking into the business should know one thing about me. I walked into my career . . .

literally. I was visiting some friends in the Village and somebody told me the Campbell's Soup guy (Andy Warhol) was making a movie in one of the apartments. So we went down to watch and next thing I know I'm being asked to be in the thing. They want me to talk to this guy on camera, then strip down to my shorts and teach him how to wrestle. It was such a joke. I couldn't believe anybody would ever pay to see such a thing. When the film opened in 1969, my picture was in all the ads. I made seven more films with Warhol and Paul Morrissey before I split and decided to make a career on my own. My unusual fame as an "underground film star" provided this troubled kid from Queens a chance to see the world.

So how can you take advice from a guy who seems to have had everything given to him? Young people come up to me now and tell me I was so lucky because I had the Warhol thing. Yeah, I was lucky. I probably would have ended up in prison if I hadn't clicked with the Warhol people. But my brother was given a chance to be in the movies and my son was given a chance years later, and they just didn't want to continue doing it. It was too boring for them. I put in the five years of strangeness and bullshit and boredom and listening to stuff that I sometimes thought was insane. I stuck with it, took advantage of it, and came to a point where I realized that what seemed insane wasn't so insane after all.

Maybe the advice I can give to young people from my own experience is that when you make a decision to get a job, stay there. You only get to a better position in work by staying with the work. Nobody's going to fault a guy for moving on if a good opportunity comes up, but people switch jobs these days for the perks, for bragging rights, and their life's work suffers.

It's hard to think about a life's work when you're young. It's a tough sell to have someone older tell you what you should be doing or what you should be thinking about. You've got to be allowed to make your own mistakes to find out what's important to you. Maybe find out that looking like a beautiful movie star doesn't make you one.

Realize, too, that the kind of beauty people tend to admire is the kind of beauty that only people outside yourself can recognize. Trust me, if it's you who decides you're beautiful simply because of the way you look, you're not going to enrich your life by stroking yourself. It's like masturbating in the corner. You're not really going to fall in love with your hand. If you do, you deserve each other. Life is about relationships, about having a relationship with another human being where ideas about surface beauty don't matter. When we ask that big question of why we were put here, it's a lot about getting along with our fellow men, not limiting ourselves to fantasy.

People need to know that we need each other. Beauty is fun. It has its place. But don't mistake it for self-worth. If you have to be beautiful, then do beautiful things for someone other than yourself.

Camille Paglia at her first teaching job at Bennington College in 1973: green corduroy Edwardian jacket, Marlboros, signature pinky ring, and Keith Richards shag.
Photo by Kristen Lippincott

Camille Paglia
Author, critic

WORDS TO LIVE BY
Maxims and Commandments from the Stars of Life, Art, and Pop

Like the restless youth of England and Northern Europe during Romanticism, my generation, born just after World War II (America's so-called "baby boom"), rebelled against authority and social conformism and often turned away from organized religion. We sought wisdom, guidance, and the meaning of life from figures outside the mainstream—poets, folksingers, activists, astrologers, gurus. From adolescence, I began collecting and reciting pithy maxims, paradoxes, and campy sallies from history, religion, high art, and pop culture. Here's a sampling of fifty quotations that fascinated me in my student years and still echo in my mind like bossy voices from the beyond.

"All things flow."

— Heraclitus

"I came, I saw, I conquered."

— Julius Caesar

"Render unto Caesar the things which are Caesar's; and unto God, the things that are God's."

— Jesus Christ

"There are more things in heaven and earth, Horatio, than are dreamt of in your philosophy."

— Shakespeare's Hamlet

"The whole visible world is only an imperceptible dot in nature's ample bosom."

—Blaise Pascal, Pensées

* * * * * * *

From WILLIAM BLAKE, *The Marriage of Heaven and Hell:*

"Drive your cart and your plow over the bones of the dead."

"The road of excess leads to the palace of wisdom."

"Exuberance is Beauty."

"If the doors of perception were cleansed every thing would appear to man as it is, infinite."

* * * * * * *

"Society never advances. It recedes as fast on one side as it gains on the other. . . . Society acquires new arts and loses old instincts."

— Ralph Waldo Emerson, Self-Reliance

"The eye is the first circle; the horizon which it forms is the second."

— Ralph Waldo Emerson, Circles

* * * * * * *

From Lewis Carroll,

"I've a right to think."
> — Alice in *Alice's Adventures in Wonderland*

"When *I* use a word, it means just what I choose it to mean—neither more, nor less."
> — Humpty Dumpty in *Through the Looking-Glass*

"Queens never make bargains."
> — the Red Queen in *Through the Looking-Glass*

"It isn't etiquette to cut any one you've been introduced to. Remove the joint!"
> — the Red Queen to Alice when she tries to carve a leg of mutton

* * * * * * *

From Oscar Wilde:

"People who count their chickens before they are hatched act very wisely since chickens run about so absurdly that it is impossible to count them accurately."

"Football is all very well as a game for rough girls, but it is hardly suitable for delicate boys."

"It is absurd to divide people into good and bad. People are either charming or tedious."

Camille Paglia

"Nowadays people know the price of everything and the value of nothing."

"Philanthropic people lose all sense of humanity. It is their distinguishing characteristic."

"All art is immoral."

"To live is the rarest thing in the world. Most people exist, that is all."

"He to whom the present is the only thing that is present, knows nothing of the age in which he lives."

"To love oneself is the beginning of a life-long romance."

"Only dull people are brilliant at breakfast."

"A mask tells us more than a face."

"Education is an admirable thing, but it is well to remember from time to time that nothing that is worth knowing can be taught."

"One should either be a work of art, or wear a work of art."

"Beauty is a form of Genius."

* * * * * * *

"Frankly, my dear, I don't give a damn."

— Rhett Butler to Scarlett O'Hara in Gone With the Wind

"Tomorrow is another day!"

— Scarlett O'Hara to herself in Gone With the Wind

"Once a tramp, always a tramp."

— Ingrid Bergman to Cary Grant at a Rio café in Notorious

"Fasten your seat belts—it's going to be a bumpy night!"

— Margo Channing (Bette Davis) to her guests in All About Eve

"So let it be written, so let it be done."

— Yul Brynner as Pharaoh in The Ten Commandments

"People who are very beautiful make their own laws."

— Tennessee Williams, The Roman Spring of Mrs. Stone

"Live, live! Life is a banquet, and most poor suckers are starving to death."

— Mame Dennis (Rosalind Russell) in Auntie Mame

"Stir, never shake—it bruises the gin."

— ten-year-old Patrick Dennis mixing martinis in Auntie Mame

"I saw the best minds of my generation destroyed by madness, starving hysterical naked."

— Allen Ginsberg, Howl

"There is a fifth dimension beyond that which is known to man. It is a dimension as vast as space and as timeless as infinity. It is the middle ground between light and shadow, between science and superstition, and it lies between the pit of man's fears and the summit of his knowledge. This is the dimension of imagination. It is an area we call the Twilight Zone."

— Rod Serling, creator and host of The Twilight Zone

"What if everything is an illusion and nothing exists? In that case I definitely overpaid for my carpet."

— Woody Allen, Without Feathers

"You don't need a weatherman to know which way the wind blows."

— Bob Dylan, "Subterranean Homesick Blues"

"Twenty years of schooling, and they put you on the day shift."

— Bob Dylan, ditto

"To live outside the law, you must be honest."

— Bob Dylan, "Absolutely Sweet Marie"

"Hey! You! Get off of my cloud!"

— the Rolling Stones, December's Children

"Think for yourself."

— the Beatles, Rubber Soul

"Gimme some truth!"

    — John Lennon, <u>Imagine</u>

"You've got to pick up every stitch."

    — Donovan, "Season of the Witch"

"Respect yourself."

    — the Staple Singers

"Love is a battlefield."

    — Pat Benatar, <u>Live from Earth</u>

"Take your passion, and make it happen."

    — Irena Cara, "Flashdance"

Bettie Page
Legendary pin-up

Show your parents that you love them by thanking them for all the good things they do for you.

Stop thinking you know it all; you will discover as you get older that you have much to learn.

Bettie Page

Judith Butler
Philosopher

Doubting Love

On occasion when I am getting to know someone—when someone seeks to know me or, indeed, find in me the occasion for love—I am asked what my idea of love is, and I always founder. There are clearly those who have their ideas of love, who enter into their conversations, their letters, their ini-

"Lucy and Linda, liplocked," from the "I can't afford Terry Richardson" series by James L. Harmon.
Photo © James L. Harmon

tial encounters with an idea of love in mind. This is admirable in a way. And I am somewhat embarrassed by the fact that I have no answer, and that I cannot, in the moment of potential seduction, offer an entrancing view of love to offer the one with whom I speak. There are those—and I imagine Jean-Luc Nancy, the French philosopher who authored an essay called "Shattered Love," to be among them—who might argue that the *idea* of love is an assault against ideation itself. One knows love somehow only when all one's ideas are destroyed, and this becoming unhinged from what one knows is the paradigmatic sign of love. Again, in the face of such views, I am full of admiration and I think that the people who believe that love shatters the idea of love are the ones who truly know what love is, who have love, who have done it, undergone it, had it done. In a way, they are sure of love. They have their certainty.

I am known to be a skeptic, if I am known at all, and so it's with some trepidation that I write here about my own doubt. I am, if anything, a secular Kierkegaardian when it comes to love. But Freud is also my guide. He is the one who writes, "A man who doubts his own love may, or rather, must doubt every lesser thing" (*SE*, X, 241). And this is the line I return to in my life, a line that cannot be read once, at least not by me. Freud is making a statement, but he is, implicitly, delivering as well a warning and an admonition. The one who doubts his own love will find himself doubting every lesser thing, but is every lesser thing the same as every other thing? Is there something that one cannot doubt if one has doubted one's own love? Or if one has doubted one's own love, then is that the same as doubting oneself, the sense of self that we derive from its essential dispossession in love? If one is doubting every lesser thing because one has doubted one's love, then that means one has lost an anchor of certainty, a firm epistemological ground. The sentence contains a certain hesitation that calls to be read: that man "may, or rather, must doubt every lesser thing." So it seems at first to Freud that doubting one's own love, but then he stops, corrects himself, and leaves his self-correction there on the page for us to read, as if reading the slide from "may" to "must" compounds its effect, dramatizes the foreclosure of possibility that follows from such a procedure. Freud's is an understated correction, but it nevertheless carries a tone of severity. There is no way around it: If you doubt your own love, you will be compelled to doubt every lesser thing, and if there is no greater thing than love, you will be compelled to doubt every other thing, which means that nothing, really nothing, will be undoubted by you.

But there is still so much to understand, and I am slow here, and I ask too many questions, too many for my own good, surely too many for the good of love. Freud tells us that it is a "man" who find himself in this predicament, doubting love, doubting lesser things. Is this a problem of manhood? Is it men who doubt when certainty is at hand? Is it part of manhood itself to call into question the affective basis of one's very self, what one feels, what one knows on the basis of what one feels? Is this business of doubting love one that men engage in, and do women who doubt become "men" of a certain kind? Are we suddenly elevated to Cartesian status, those who find that feeling in general induces a radical uncertainty about what we do and can do and know? And now watch as I raise it only to move on to another question, one that pertains to something perhaps more fundamental.

But perhaps the most important question I ask of this prodigious sentence from Freud has to do with what it might mean, after all, to doubt one's own love. If one doubts one's own love, then does that mean that one does not know to whom it belongs, or to whom it ought to belong? Does it mean that one does not know whether one loves when one thinks that one does, or says that one does? Or does it mean that one does not know whether one is wise in the moment of love, whether love is something that might be relied upon to show one the way. If we came away from Freud's claim with the conclusion that one should never doubt one's own love, that matters will become perilous if one does, then I think we are making a mistake. For surely the founder of psychoanalysis cannot be telling us that our love is always wise, that it always furnishes the grounds by which we might have certain knowledge of our world. We are usually fooled by love, find ourselves repeating older scenes in what appears as novel and unprecedented, find ourselves returned to older patterns of self after ecstatic outbursts of love, or one comes to think about one's ecstasy in new ways, wondering whether this is ecstasy, whether this is love, doubting, doubting.

And though it seems clear that one who enters analysis also enters into a scene of love, that love, that transference, is but the schema of one's love reflected back in ways one wished one never saw. For this understanding to occur, one immobilizes the body in order to speak, and one never exchanges a touch with the one before whom one speaks, before whom one performs one's silence. So it is a kind of love, but it is one that restrains itself radically, and which bespeaks that restraint, thematizes that restraint, works for its fecundity, when it works. It is not exactly a model for love, but it is a relationship, a pure potential that takes on a certain structure in time.

And given that so much mental suffering stems from the belief that love of one sort or another is not possible, this scene of pure impossibility, of no actuality, can open up a horizon that one previously took to be closed. Indeed, the question of how to translate from analysis to life is another one, and there are no recipes here. But analysis has some part of life in it (though it is not life), and life has some part of analysis in it (though it is not analysis).

It would seem that for Freud the goal is not to doubt one's own love, to come to have certainty in it, and to somehow know oneself in the dispossession that love provides. I am the one who loses myself here, in this way, under these conditions; who finds the following irresistible; who falls then and there; who wants, who idealizes, who pursues; who cannot forget this or that kind of thing, wants it again, cannot stop wanting it easily; who wants to be pursued, or to become unforgettable, irreplaceable. One finds that love is not a state, a feeling, a disposition, but an exchange, uneven, fraught with history, with ghosts, with longings that are more or less legible to those who try to see one another with their own faulty vision.

If one becomes somewhat savvy about one's love—"ah yes, there goes my love again, what will bring forth this time? What havoc will it wreak?"—does this mean that one ceases to doubt it, or that one knows it with certainty for all time? Or is this the distance that one takes from what one cannot do, an instance of the doubt that goes along with love? We might think Freud is saying that to doubt one's own love is to doubt it in a very fundamental way, to call the most important matters into question, and to not let assumptions go unquestioned. It is, in a way, to become philosophical in and about one's passions. And this does not mean that one ceases to live them or that one kills them by thinking them into the ground. On the contrary, one lives them, and seeks to know them, but only by bringing one's questions into the practice of love itself. I cannot pretend to know myself at the moment of love, but I cannot pretend to fully know myself. I must neither vacate the knowledge that I have—the knowledge, after all, that will make me a better lover—and I cannot be the one who knows everything in advance—which would make me proud and, finally, loveable. Love always returns us to what we do and do not know. We have no other choice than to become shaken by doubt, and to persist with what we can know when we can know it.

Roger Scruton
Philosopher

Advice to Those Who Come After Us

Pleasures go stale, but happiness is always fresh and fulfilling. Even if you are only interested in yourself, therefore, you should ask how happiness is obtained and how, once obtained, it can be kept. The most important ingredient in happiness is self-esteem: the knowledge that it is good to be what you are. This knowledge requires the distinction between good and bad. And this is not learned from judging, yourself, but from judging others and being judged by them. To be happy, therefore, you must see yourself as others might, and find no obstacle to approbation. What you admire in others, you should strive to imitate in yourself.

This is a fruitful thought experiment. Take all the things that you want to do, and ask yourself, Would it endear another to me, to know that he did them? Consider infidelity. Why is it that, in all the great literature of love, the reader finds himself instinctively on the side of the faithful, and unable to take the betrayer to heart? If you are moved to sympathy for the adulterer, say, it is almost invariably because the writer or artist has portrayed him or her as pursuing an extramarital but faithful love against the background of a marriage imposed by force, convention, or habit. This is what Tolstoy does in *Anna Karenina,* or Wagner in *Tristan and Isolde.* The problematic cases are problematic for this very reason. Does our heart, in the end, really go out to Emma Bovary in Flaubert's novel, or to Don Giovanni in Mozart's opera?

Consider all your character traits in this light and you will soon learn which ones should be amended; violent temper, injustice, cowardice, and gross self-indulgence all place an insuperable obstacle before our affections. So let them place an obstacle before the affection that you naturally feel for yourself.

Once you begin to think in this moralized way about your life, you will recognize an important distinction not only between the good and the bad, but between the good and the nice. Nice people may be good, but in many cases niceness is a mask behind which self-interest negotiates an easy passage to its target. Nice people may charm us, do their best to get us on their side, encumber us with easily offered and cost-free expressions of affection. But it does not follow that we can trust them to help us in the real emergency, or to make sacrifices on our behalf or on behalf of anyone. For this something deeper is required—the thing that we know as virtue.

Aristotle argued that true friendship requires virtue in those who are joined by it. He meant that friendship is not just a good and a part of happiness; it is also laden with duties and obligations and cannot be sustained without cost. The cost is worthwhile, but it may not be pleasant. Virtue is the disposition to meet that cost from your own resources: to take risks on your friend's behalf, to stand up for him in difficulties, to expose yourself to obloquy when justice requires. Without courage, wisdom, and justice, therefore, friendship is only a ghost.

To retain happiness is not so hard, if our faithful companions are beside us. They are our comfort in adversity and the partners of our joys. All promiscuous affection tends to sever these lasting relationships of love and trust, and although this may bring rewards in terms of instant pleasure, it erodes the foundations of esteem. But lasting loves and friendships imply that grief will one day afflict us. And grief is a mourning, not only for the other, but for the self. We die with those whom we love, and this rehearsal for our final exit is one that many find hard to bear.

Here is another thought experiment. Imagine your own death, in a world where no one loves you or regrets your passing, but in which you have had your fair share of instant pleasures. Now imagine your death in a world where you are mourned and regretted, and where images of your character and deeds are treasured by those whom you leave behind. Soon you will come to prefer this second world, not only in the future when you have left it, but in the present, when death is only approaching at its accustomed pace. And you will come to see that there are worse things than death, and that, in the end, death is not the most grievous of your losses. Far worse is to live too long, clinging to a life that has lost its enchantment. (Janacek's opera the *Makropulos Case*, based on a play by Karel Capek, makes this point beautifully.) This is part of what Nietzsche meant in recommending "timely death." And beware of the health fanatics and the cult of youth, which tell you to keep the pristine shell of a human being while the inner soul goes rotten. Grow mature with confidence and old with dignity, and accept your death as the price. It is well worth it.

In all ages, it seems to me, the advice that I have given holds good. It depends for its validity on no religion, no abstract metaphysics, no rehearsal through ritual and myth. But it also provides the secret meaning of those things, and perhaps, when our present culture has finally lost all hold on the imagination, another will come in place of it which will enable us once again to experience these moral truths as immediate, obvious, and comforting. Open your heart to that possibility; there is nothing to lose.

Ken Kesey
Writer

Don't say it. It's too hard to take it back. I've seen too many loves sundered by too much needless honesty. These psychological ding-dongs who tell people to speak their minds to their mates, to vent their spleens—what do they accomplish? All they produce is a lot of lonely self-righteous minds and ventilated spleens.

Gene Wolfe
Writer

God's creation is a single seamless whole—those seven words are all that are needed to convey the most important principle I can ever expound to you. In L. Sprague de Camp's biography of Robert E. Howard, he relates that Howard, a good amateur boxer, had the odd habit of shadowboxing as he walked along whenever he felt himself un-

No Fear: Gene Wolfe, age 22.

observed. In truth it isn't an odd habit at all. All boxers, amateur (I too used to be one) and professional, do it.

Other things are the same. One of publisher Tom Doherty's daughters often gripes that her father thinks everything can be thought of in terms of baseball. And so it can. Infielders can be seen going down for imaginary grounders and throwing phantom strikes to first. This method—*rehearsal*—is the most vital technique I can pass along. It will banish fears and bring you many victories. I guarantee it. Are you going to an important meeting? Write yourself a little play. And, yes, I mean actually write it. What will you say as you come in? What will that frightening person across the desk say? What arguments can you bring to bear, and how can you best phrase them? What counters are to be anticipated? How can you parry them without degrading the discussion to a battle? Put it all in that little play. When I'm stuck on a novel or a story, I write the review I'd like it to get. The technique is universally applicable.

History is the rehearsal of the race. And since you're reading this book you presumably realize already that—and here is the most vital information I have to give you—appearances in life change far more than realities, that the counsels of Socrates remain valid today despite the obvious deterioration suffered by civilization over the past 2,400 years. Things were simpler back then, and thus easier to see clearly. Or perhaps the people of Greece in that age, living so near the edge, fending off empires on nerve and a handful of olives, looked harder.

Never forget that Shakespeare wrote with a feather. The steel pen was an improvement on that feather, the fountain pen an improvement on that quill, the typewriter an improvement on the fountain pen, the electric typewriter an improvement on the typewriter, and the electronic typewriter an improvement on the electric typewriter. Now we have computers and word-processing programs.

But we do not have better plays, and in fact we do not have plays nearly as good. Nine times out of ten success follows the skillful, imaginative use of such simple techniques as rehearsal—ours or theirs.

Before I leave you, I'd like to recommend three particular rehearsals for your careful consideration. David, son of Jesse, and Miyamoto Musashi actually *were* sword-swinging adventurers of the kind Robert E. Howard wrote about, and both left behind them books of their own—books for which we would pay fortunes if we did not already possess them. If you've read them already, read them again.

James Butler Hickok, better known as Wild Bill, left us no book but he did leave us his advice. He may well have been the premier gunfighter of all time. His shoot-out with Dave Tutt, held in the town square of Springfield, Missouri, before hundreds of witnesses, was the origin of all those high-noon gunfights staged in the dusty streets of Hollywood back lots. How good was he, really? He was murdered by a drifter named Jack McCall—shot in the back of the head while he was playing cards. When his dead body hit the floor, he had both guns out and one cocked.

But before that dark day came, someone (some time-traveler, perhaps) actually asked Wild Bill Hickok how to do it, how to come out of a real gunfight under your own power. His advice, Wild Bill's advice, is the last, or almost the last, I will leave with you. This because I have seen so many fail through timidity, and so few through being over-bold. Just seven more words: *Wild Bill Hickcok said, "Don't be a-sceered."* Everything can be referred to everything. Remember always that God's shirt was, and is, one seamless whole, for which once we cast lots.

Gene Wolfe

Mary Gaitskill
Writer

My advice here is very specific and practicable. It is advice I wish someone had given me as forcefully as I'm about to give it now: When your parents are dying, you should go be with them. You should spend as much time as you can. This may seem obvious; you would be surprised how difficult it can be. It is less difficult if you have a good relationship with the parent or, even if you don't, if you're old enough to have lost friends and to have seriously considered your own death. Even so, it may be more difficult than you think. You may have young children that you can't leave alone, you may be sick yourself, you may find yourself strangely focused on completing a task at work—you may simply not want to believe it's happening. If you are a young person who has had a bad relationship with your parent, it's a nightmare of anger, confusion, and guilt. Even if you hate them, you may still not want to believe it's happening. Whoever you are, if the death is prolonged, it's harder still. If it happens too fast for you to get there, that is a whole other topic, another kind of difficulty. But, if there is time, you've got to go be with them, for as long as you can.

I'm certain that there are people to whom this general directive does not apply, and I don't mean this as a rebuke to those people. However, it is one of the only general directives I stand behind. Even if your parents have been abusive, physically or emotionally, they are part of you in a way that goes beyond personality or even character. Maybe "beyond" isn't the right word. They are part of you in a way that runs beneath the daily self. They have passed an essence to you. This essence may not be recognizable; your parents may have made its raw matter into something so different than what you have made of it that it seems you are nothing alike. That they have given you this essence may be no virtue of theirs—they may not have chosen to do so. (It may not be biological either; all I say here I would say about adoptive as well as birth parents.)

If nothing else, you should go be with them just to acknowledge that they will soon be gone, that you will no longer be that person's child in the sense you once were. I have a friend whose mother physically abused him when he was a child, and who has continued to bully and hector him (in increasingly comical ways) as an old lady. There is no question that he'll be with her when she's dying. This may be partly because he recognizes that he got his tenacity and fire from her. It's also because in honoring his mother he is honoring the hard truth that we know nothing about who we are or what our lives mean. Nothing makes this plainer than being in the presence of a dying person for any length of time. Death makes human beings seem like very small containers that are packed so densely we can only be aware of a fraction of what's inside us from moment to moment. Being in the presence of death can break you open, disgorging feelings that are deeper and more powerful than anything you thought you knew. If you have had a loving, clear relationship with your parent, this experience probably won't be quite as wrenching. There may in fact be moments of pure tenderness, even exaltation. But you might still have to watch your parent appear to break, mentally and physically, disintegrating into something you can no longer recognize. In some ways this is terrible—many people find it absolutely so. There is another side to it, though: In witnessing this seeming breakage, we are glimpsing the part of our parents that doesn't translate in human terms, that which we know nothing about, and which the human container is too small to give shape to.

On good behavior: A doe-eyed Mary Gaitskill.

It might not happen this way. Your parent may be lucid right up until the end. They might talk to you about how much they love you, they might talk to you about taking care of the garbage, or taxes, or socks. How pissed they are at their neighbor—maybe even how

Mary Gaitskill

pissed they are at you. The variety of possible experience makes absurd all but the most general advice. Knowing how to respond from moment to moment requires a lot of attention: Your physical touch may be calming to them or it might be agitating. They might want you to sing to them, but at some point words might be too stimulating; they might just want to hear melodic sounds. Pay attention to their responses, stuff like whether they're tensing up or relaxing. Ask them what they want, even when it comes to little things like whether they want you sitting on the bed or not. If they can't talk, ask for a nonverbal sign. I like to think that even if you can't figure out exactly what they mean, and do everything wrong, they'll still feel you there, being the well-meaning boob you always were, and that the familiarity might be the most comforting thing of all.

Knowing your feelings is hard too because there's so much emotion, it's hard to tell which is truest. Part of you might want to leave right away; part of you might want to stay forever. That's why I advised that you stay "for as long as you can." What that means will vary with each person, with the needs of the parent and the other relations. A day might be enough, or it might take a whole month. If it's a prolonged situation, it might be good to leave for a few days and come back. Those decisions are so personal they are beyond the scope of my advice—except my advice to pay close attention to yourself. If you feel, *To hell with this, I'm getting out,* don't worry—there's room for that. Maybe in fact you should leave. But before you do, be sure that voice is not shouting down a truer one. When your parents die, you will never see them again. You might think you understand that, but until it happens, you don't. They say that you come into the world alone and that you leave alone too. But you aren't born alone; your mother is with you, maybe your father too. Their presence may have been loving, it may have been demented, it may have been both. But they were with you. When they are dying, remember that. And go be with them.

Richard Powers
Writer

Never forget what you were born knowing: That this fluke, single, huge, cross-indexed, thermodynamic experiment of a story that the world has been inventing to tell itself at bedtime is still in embryo. It's not even the outline of a synopsis of notes toward a rough draft yet. Buy the plot some time; take in more, consume less, recycle everything; book-keep all hidden costs; find out where you have been set down; lobby for a smarter market; get rid of your car and travel as widely as you can (yeah, walk: what the hell); try to say a little more than you mean; carry a pocket encyclopedia (ask for the one without packaging) and when the entry on "Diffusion Constant" says, "For more information, see 'Pastry War,'" see "Pastry War."

Shake yourself loose of the local. Take a full look at the worst. Acknowledge the figures: the runaway birthrates, the irreversible extinctions and ruined habitats, the meaningless economies fueled by waste, the exported shooting wars and their covert causes, the widening gulf between north and south, the nations on the brink, the child suicides, the built-in insanity of the race, the native immigrant denied due process in the next apartment over. Then work at whatever comes to hand. Useful or not, it makes no difference. Jumping in is the only calculus that emergency ever allows.

And in those years when you cannot believe that even this infinitely unlikely script is leading anywhere, never deny that you still want it to. Wait for hope's replacement. Even fear has its uses; "meticulous" originally meant "afraid," once upon a time. Stand still and tick off the smallest tip of the entire catalog in your head. Pleasure in existence is a moral imperative.

Remember what your driver's education teacher (that enormous, balding, high-voiced man, at this minute riding the death seat beside sixteen-year-olds worldwide from Peru to Kenya, foot covering the jimmied-up auxiliary brake, hand clasping the dash for dear life, sweating it out until imminent retirement) always told you:

Good God, slow down.

Leave yourself an out.

Aim high in steering.

Get the Big Picture.

* * * * * * * * *

Michael Thomas Ford
Writer

Scraps

I am almost thirty-three years old—the same age Jesus Christ was when he was crucified and only two years younger than Buddha when he became enlightened. This is not good news, particularly as I spend most of my time not in attempting to save the world or achieve inner peace but in trying to think up excuses to give my editors for why my manuscripts are late. Sometimes I do laundry, order takeout, or putter around in the garden, but most of the time I just wonder what it all means and why I bother.

I don't recall ever receiving any advice from anyone when I was growing up. I wish I had some good story about an ol' Irish grandmother who told me something that has stayed with me through the years, or perhaps an uplifting tale featuring an encouraging teacher who shaped my destiny with a few immortal words. But I don't. My Irish grandmother was more interested in listening to books on tape and complaining about the weather than she was in dispensing wisdom, and my teachers just wanted to get home to a good stiff drink after their days with us. It's probably just as well. I didn't believe anything I was told when I was younger, and mostly I've forgotten it all anyway.

So after thirty-three years of living, I must shamefully admit that I don't really have anything particularly helpful to say about how to do things. Occasionally I've thought that, finally, I understand what it's all about and I know where I'm going. But I'm always wrong. I admire people who choose, or even fall into, a particular ideology, spiritual path, or twelve-step program that gives them direction. I am in awe of people who are confident that certain things work while others don't. I'm just not one of those people. I embrace ideas one day and discard them the next. I can easily convince myself that completely opposing arguments are both correct. I do not have a philosophy.

That's not to say that I haven't learned a few things. I have, although usually by accident. And when I do I write them on scraps of paper and stick them in a box that sits on a shelf in my office. Every so often I take the little pieces of paper out of the box and look at them. Holding them in my hands makes me feel as if I've progressed a little bit and that I'm not as hopeless as I often believe I am. Then I put the scraps away and go back to coming up with excuses for not working on my manuscripts.

I said I was progressing, not that I was getting very far.

Sometimes I choose a piece of paper at random and read it, hoping that its message will be in some way helpful at that particular moment, like those eerily spot-on fortune cookies you sometimes get. Usually it isn't. But occasionally it's exactly what I need to hear at the time, so perhaps it's not an entirely useless system. Assuming that to be the case, this morning I picked ten scraps at random. Here is what turned up. Do with them what you will.

1. You do not need to learn French. I took French for eight years. I cannot speak a word of it. I cannot buy a train ticket to Lyon, or ask Jeanine where to buy oranges, or comment on the beauty of Provence—at least not in French. Sometimes I feel guilty about this. I also sometimes feel guilty about not being able to build kitchen cabinets, or read a compass, or make my own pasta. I wrote this to remind myself that there is no reason at all why I should be able to do these things. If I want to learn how to do them, that's fine. But otherwise there are carpenters, forest rangers, and cooks who do know how to do those things and who do them better than I ever could. I should allow them that distinction, and gladly.

2. People who are mean to waitpeople are probably not very nice. I don't have scientific proof of this, but I can assure you that it's true. They are not people who will make your life better, and it's best to rid yourself of them as quickly as possible. I have never met someone who will speak rudely to a waiter and who will then treat other people with kindness. I had an agent once who yelled at a waitress while we were having lunch. As I listened to her complain about her salad I realized that every time she called me I got a stomachache. I fired her (over the phone, when I got home). My new agent is very nice to waiters, does not order salads, and I love hearing from him.

3. There is nothing so pressing that you can't take the dog for a walk. I have a Labrador who likes to go for walks. Lots of walks. I have lived with him for eight years, which means that at four outings a day I have been on approximately 11,680 walks. I don't always feel like taking Roger on walks. Sometimes I even try explaining to him that I'm far too busy with deadlines to go anywhere. But inevitably he doesn't listen, and whines until I am forced to abandon what I'm doing so that he can drag me down the street to the park. When I do, and I see how happy it makes him, I feel better myself and I find that my writing is much more enjoyable when I go back to it. So take your dog out a lot. If you don't have a dog, I feel sorry for you. Everyone should have a dog.

4. You are allowed to like Bruce Willis movies. I love films where things explode. I also love television, pop music, and fast-food restaurants. These things are wonderful. So are opera, museums, and theater. But I don't trust people who wrinkle their noses when you say your favorite show is *Buffy the Vampire Slayer* or who appear shocked when you mention reading Jackie Collins novels or listening to ABBA. These things are fun, and you need fun. Not everything in life has to be deep and meaningful. Spending three hours watching the Oscars to see what people are wearing is just as legitimate as sitting through *La Boheme*. Plus, you can have snacks.

5. Just because a relationship ends does not mean it was a failure. It bothers me when people say things like, "I can't believe I wasted three years of my life with him." Time spent with someone else is only wasted if you didn't learn something from it. You don't have to be friends with your ex, but you should be thankful for whatever your time together taught you about yourself and about what you want from your life.

6. Take chances. I know that sounds simplistic, but it's harder than you think. I seem to pick this scrap a lot, probably because I need to be reminded of this on a fairly regular basis. The older you get, the more excuses you come up with for why you can't quit your job and spend three months writing that screenplay or why it's ridiculous for you to even think about running in that marathon. Of course it's all a fear of failure. But failing is a lot better than wondering what might have happened. If you're pretty sure something isn't going to kill you, there's no reason not to give it a shot.

7. Eat cheesecake. I remember the day I wrote this one. I had gone to the gym and was feeling awful about how I looked. I came home and read one of my favorite passages by Anne LaMott. In it she describes trying on a dress for an upcoming date and asking her friend Pammy if she looks fat in it. Pammy, who is dying of cancer, says, "Annie, I really don't think you have that kind of time." I still go to the gym, but now I'm realistic about it. The world isn't going to change if I have perfect abs, and it's not worth denying myself something I like so that I can wear size 32 jeans. Thanks, Pammy. And Annie, if you're reading this, that was me who left the message on your answering machine thanking you for writing that book. I think of you every time I eat cheesecake.

8. It's good to say no. The best day of my life was when I realized that, for the most part, I don't have to do things I don't want to do. I don't have to go to parties just because I like the hosts. I don't have to celebrate holidays just because everyone else is. I don't have to write things I don't want to just because I'm afraid of annoying the editor by refusing. My time is my own. I'm not going to spend it wishing I were doing something else.

9. You are not responsible for the rest of the world. I sponsor two children, one in the United States and one in Indonesia. I do it because it doesn't cost very much and because maybe it will help them somehow. I also recycle and give money to the Friends Committee to Abolish the Death Penalty. But that's about it. I used to want to join every group that worked for something I believe in. But then reading all those mailings and trying to divvy up my annual contributions budget between 327 different organizations just got to be too much. So I picked a couple I think work and I stick with them. You can't save everything or everyone. All you can do is your little bit. Someone else can worry about the whales. I've got Indonesia covered.

10. You won't know what happens to you when you die until you die. I write quite a bit about faith and spirituality. Because of this, people like to ask me what I believe. I don't have an answer for them. The fact is, until it happens I'm not going to know what death is all about. In the meantime, I'm not going to worry about it. There are better things to do, like eat cheesecake.

Mark Dery
Cultural critic

The Sunshine Syndrome:
Portrait of the Artist as a
Jaundiced Don Diego

[Author's Note: *Uneasy in the role of gener-
ational oracle offering sage counsel to the
Leaders of Tomorrow, I've decided to channel my teenaged self. The following autobiographical essay, equal parts true confession
and comic sociology, is a homily on the
importance of putting as much mileage as
possible between you and the mind-cramping
confines of Middle America. That, and the
importance of acting on your subversive
impulses while you're still young (unless, of
course, they involve black helicopters, bomb
threats, or Jenna Bush).*—Mark Dery]

Jethro Tull T-shirt, David
Cassidy hair, and sun belt
angst: Mark Dery in the
smiley-face '70s.

I grew up in Chula Vista, a little dingleberry of a city clinging to San
Diego's outskirts, just a spit away from Tijuana. Chula Vista is best
known—albeit erroneously—as the site of James Oliver Huberty's
1984 shooting spree in a McDonald's. Actually, that happened in
San Ysidro, a hard-luck border town south of Chula Vista. Huberty,
an unemployed security guard, gun nut, and camo-clad Rambo
wannabe, is a poster boy for what pop psychologists have called "the
sunshine syndrome."

A volatile mix of dead-end anomie and free-floating rage, the
sunshine syndrome is what kicks in when the career loser who's
gambled his last chance on "the golden land where every day the
world is born anew" (Joan Didion) wakes up to the fact that the
streets aren't paved with gold.[1] California is where the open road,

with its seductive promise of a clean slate and a second chance, turns into the road to nowhere, like the unfinished freeway ramp that was a local landmark during my boyhood, its concrete arc ending in midair, a Pharaonic monument to the dream of driving off the edge of the map. (This archetypal sight has resurfaced in the dream life of the Golden State. In the '70s, a band of ironists known as the LA Fine Arts Squad immortalized the image in a trompe l'oeil mural of a freeway ending in midair over the ocean, its concrete foundations pounded by the surf.) California is where the American faith in endless frontiers and boundless possibilities finally runs out of gas—a place, wrote Didion, "in which a boom mentality and a sense of Chekovian loss meet in uneasy suspension; in which the mind is troubled by some buried but ineradicable suspicion that things had better work here, because here, beneath that immense bleached sky, is where we run out of continent."[2]

It's also where the Mexican colonists, not to mention the Native Americans of Ishi and *Island of the Blue Dolphins* fame, were run *off* the continent. San Diego's ambassador of goodwill is Don Diego, a good-naturedly racist caricature of a Disneyfied Mexican who greets all tourists with the same beaming bonhomie that his ranchero forebears doubtless showed toward the invading Yankees, who repaid them for their hospitality by taking the old Mexican saying *"mi casa es su casa"* literally. James Oliver Huberty is Don Diego's distorted doppelganger, the sociopathic dark side of California dreamin'. If the region's travel-brochure image is Disneyland and the endless summer of Beach Boys myth, its private face is the summer of fear inflicted on LA by Richard Ramirez, the "Night Stalker" killer whose deadpan, surfer-dude response to his death sentence was quintessentially Californian: "See you in Disneyland."

Some writers are steeped in a sense of place. My writing is informed by Southern California's placelessness, its geography of nowhere. Despite its longstanding status as a mirage in the Desert of the Real—a delirium of Hollywood special effects, theme-parked cityscapes, steroidal muscleboys, and surgically enhanced beach babes—Los Angeles can always muster a little cultural gravitas, if some is needed, by invoking its noir past (the Black Dahlia murder, Fitzgerald and Faulkner reduced to studio hacks) and Xtreme present (gangbangers, race riots). By contrast, the San Diego environs I came to know, growing up there in the '60s and '70s—cities such as Lemon Grove, La Mesa, El Cajon, San Ysidro, and of course Chula Vista—seemed not only placeless but pastless, a purgatorial horror of apartment complexes and convenience stores, churches and fast-food drive-throughs, most of them younger than I was.

My childhood memories are set against a backdrop of Taco Bells and Bible bookstores, strip malls and sprawl—the metastasis of the landscape by housing developments with mazelike streets and eerily identical dream homes. One emblematic memory is the summer I worked the first of many jobs from hell, selling peanut brittle door-to-door for what I now suspect was a front organization for the Nation of Islam. My Black Muslim employers would drive me to suburban developments light years from nowhere, where I would thread my way through a labyrinth of streets, dazed by the oven heat and disoriented by the lookalike facades of the assembly-line tract houses. The only thing moving on the shadowless, griddle-hot streets, I felt as if I'd stepped into one of those sci-fi movies where everyone but the heavily armed hero and the deranged, mutated remains of the human race have been annihilated by a viral plague or a nuclear Armageddon. I'd ring a doorbell and wait. And wait. And wait. Through the flyblown screen door, I could just make out the glow of a TV in the dark of a shaded room. Somewhere, a dog barked. Finally, I'd move on, wondering what sort of people watched TV in the middle of the day with the shades down, and why they didn't answer their doors. Flashing back to the post-apocalyptic thriller *The Omega Man*, I'd imagine the desiccated body of a housewife slumped in front of the flickering set, slowly mummifying in the desert heat. . . .

Landscapes like these were the real-life sets, when I was a kid, for the serial murders of the Candlelight Killer, a Hollywood hack's idea of a bogeyman whose signature was a guttering candle, left near his victims. In a delicious irony, California—often accused of being one big Hollywood backlot, one long theme-park dark ride—is also an incubator of mediagenic psychopaths who commit their serial murders in TV miniseries—like installments. Is it pure chance that Manson's family holed up at the Spahn movie ranch, backdrop for countless grade-B Westerns?

Chula Vista and San Diego, for me, were places to flee—dug-in enclaves of Sunbelt Babbittry with exactly the sort of zero tolerance for rebellious teenagers, bleeding-heart liberals, and troublesome blacks and Chicanos that you'd expect from a region ruled by Reagan Republicans, navy retirees, and born-again Christians. Did I mention white supremacists? The White Aryan Resistance, founded by TV repairman Tom Metzger, found fertile soil in the intellectual Mojave of Southern California.

In the '70s, Chula Vista was derided by other San Diegans as "Chulajuana" for its proximity to Tijuana and high percentage of resident "beaners" (minuses in the eyes of those in affluent zip codes like La Jolla, where the only brown faces in sight were those of the illegal immigrants who tended the gardens and cleaned the houses). In fact, the naturalized sons and daughters of Tijuana's ruling class (all of whom seemed, by some odd coincidence, to be lighter-skinned than most Mexicans) assimilated effortlessly into my school's social elite. But they were mirrored, at the other end of the class ladder, by the low-riding *cholos* and their defiantly sleazy girlfriends, with their black nail polish and their jailbait midriffs. I can still feel the dead-eyed, contemptuous stare that stopped me cold the time I stumbled onto a knot of them copping a smoke in a corner of the schoolyard. Half-remembered rumors still echo distantly in my mind, of high school guys who used "wetbacks" for target practice out among the arroyos and scrub-covered badlands of Chula Vista's canyon country.

Racism is deep in the California grain. Michael Douglas's

angry white guy in *Falling Down*, hell-bent on payback in an LA peo-
pled with immigrants, gangbangers, and freaks, is only one of the
more recent figments of the paranoid white imagination in a state
whose Midwestern settlers have never stopped circling the wagons
against the massing hordes of Mexican immigrants, Asian invaders,
and urban blacks. Douglas's D-FENS (the name says it all) is a lin-
eal descendant of Raymond Chandler's hard-boiled detective Philip
Marlowe, the "best man in his world" of greasy haired Indians who
give off the "earthy smell of the primitive man," "Jap" gardeners
who manicure the lawns of rich whites "with the usual contemptuous
expression Jap gardeners have," and "smokes" and "shines" who grin
and roll their eyes in the best Stepin Fetchit fashion when they're
not regarding Marlowe in the "dead, alien silence of another race."[3]

In recent decades, as California's whites have dreamed fitfully
of the Day of Reckoning when brown and yellow faces are in the
majority, Marlowe has had plenty of company. According to LA-
ologist Mike Davis, the visions of LA in ruins, riots, or both that
haunted the disaster fiction of the '70s were a white nightmare
about societal breakdown, tinted with xenophobia and bigotry.
They proliferated during "a period of transition in Los Angeles, as
the WASP stronghold became a cosmopolitan metropolis with an
emergent non-Anglo majority. Mexican immigrants were displac-
ing Midwesterners as the largest single 'ethnic' group, and the city
was bitterly dividing over issues of school busing, tax reform,
crime, and police abuse."[4] Similarly, the alien-invasion fantasies
that inundated pop culture in the '80s were a manifestation, says
Davis, of "the increasing visibility of immigrants from Mexico,
Central America, and East Asia in the daily life of the Los Angeles
region."[5]

Like the region's deep-rooted suspicion of intellectualism and
its knee-jerk conservatism, SoCal racism is a legacy of the hard-
scrabble Midwesterners who brought their god-fearing faith and
their rural ways to the Eden among the orange groves. There, they
built a society where, in Didion's tart assessment, "it is easy to Dial-

A-Devotion, but hard to buy a book."[6] Its idea of culture is *The Nut-cracker Suite* (a staple of the San Diego Symphony's repertoire throughout my youth); its shrine to gracious living is the Lawrence Welk Resort ("a haven for virtues, family values, and endless relaxation," in the words of its website). The Life of the Mind vaporizes on contact with San Diego backwaters like Lakeside, Santee, Poway, Otay Mesa—places where you can drive for miles without seeing a bookstore, though the god-bothering business is a growth industry, packing church parking lots with cars whose bumperstickers blare, "In Case of Rapture, Car Will Be Driverless" or "It's a Child, Not a Choice."

The soul-shriveling law-and-order conformity of the region produces antibodies like Lemon Grove homeboy and dada-punk troublemaker Boyd Rice, whose cathartic hijinx (recounted in the Re/Search book *Pranks!*) include abusing baffled customers from his hiding place in the belfry of the Taco Bell where he worked ("That's a very pudgy child. That child is overweight. If I had a child that fat I wouldn't dress it in such bright colors. . . .").[7] A high school friend of mine was a textbook example of the tropism toward rebellion encouraged by SoCal's repressive climate. Though he dropped out of school, his devout study of *The Anarchist's Cookbook* stood him in good stead: He vented his hostility against our time-warped school, where after-school attendance at pep rallies was compulsory (state law be damned), by booby-trapping our graduation. Just as our born-again valedictorian was warming to her theme—a heartfelt meditation on the timeless advice to tomorrow's leaders hidden in a Barry Manilow song—a brain-curdling barrage of booms echoed around the football stadium. Hidden among the giant chalk letters that spelled out the school name on a nearby bank of ice plant, timer-controlled M80s went off, sending dirt clods whizzing skyward and covering the capped and gowned students in dust and glory. Our valedictorian soldiered on boldly, but soon collapsed into tears, her muffled sobs reverberating through the PA amid the escalating carnage all around us, to the undisguised glee of the class of '78. Years later, he was arrested for returning, masked, to the Catholic school where he spent his unhappy elementary-school years and pie-facing the nun who was his principal tormentor. Recently, I heard from another old high school friend that he'd killed himself.

Little wonder that after college, I moved to New York and never looked back, fearful that I'd be turned into a David Hasselhoff—shaped pillar of salt. Nonetheless, I have San Diego to thank for the very fact that I am a writer. Apparently, the imp of the perverse in me needed something to push against—the cultural equivalent of isometric exercise. I found it in abundance in the unbudgeable bedrock of Southern California's native anti-intellectualism—a congenital distrust of too much thinking inherited from dustbowl drifters, bible-thumping fundies, New Age cultists, and generations of Malibu Barbies, *Baywatch* beefcake, and other votaries of the body beautiful. Growing up in SoCal shaped me as a writer, instilling in me an undying desire to beat the Devil—conservatism, bigotry, anti-intellectualism—wherever I found him.

Great beaches, though. And I'm a fan of San Diego's cherished wackos, the saucer-worshipping Uranians; its vintage stucco bungalows; its freeways, not quite as futuristic as LA's signature cloverleafs but stunning nonetheless (especially the San Diego–Coronado bridge, a gravity-defying arc of steel and concrete that launches your car into what feels like suborbital flight); and the surreal Santa Ana heat waves, indelibly etched in memories of hair-trigger tempers, spontaneous nosebleeds, grasshoppers bouncing drunkenly off the windows, and burning skies hazy with forest-fire ash.

Of course, the best thing about San Diego is Mexico, specifically Tijuana, the wonderfully seedy, obscene id to San Diego's Jesus-saves, support-your-local-sheriff superego. To this day, Tijuana remains a mecca for American teenagers and Camp Pendleton jarheads in search of switchblades, stuffed iguanas, and social diseases. Tijuana is the abiding inspiration for my literary border-crossings into the interzones of the psyche, the shady backstreets of the subconscious. In a sense, my writings on the gothic, the grotesque, the carnivalesque—in short, extremes and excess of every sort—may represent a lifelong attempt to find my way back to the nocturnal Tijuana of my adolescence, with its black-velvet paintings and its cheap tequila, the marquees on its overlit boulevards ballyhooing depraved entertainments like the one whose name I will never forget: "Bride of the Burro."

Notes

1. Joan Didion, *Slouching Toward Bethlehem* (New York: Delta, 1968), p. 28.

2. *Ibid.*, p. 172.

3. "The best man in his world": "The Simple Art of Murder," in *Chandler: Later Novels and Other Writings* (New York: The Library of America, 1995), p. 992. "The earthy smell of the primitive man": "Mandarin's Jade," in *Killer in the Rain* (New York: Ballantine Books, 1987), p. 191. "Jap" gardeners: *ibid.*, p. 217. "The dead, alien silence": "Try the Girl," in *Killer in the Rain*, p. 130.

4. Mike Davis, *Ecology of Fear: Los Angeles and the Imagination of Disaster* (New York: Vintage, 1998), p. 326.

5. *Ibid.*, p. 341.

6. Didion, *Slouching Toward Bethlehem*, p. 4.

7. *Pranks!: Re/Search #11*, ed. Andrea Juno and V. Vale (San Francisco: Re/Search Publications, 1987), p. 25.

Alexander Theroux
Poet, writer

We are essentially alone in the world. No intimacy endures forever. People can't afford to care for long. You can't have a relationship of even a month without finding a major reason to leave that person forever. Nothing's finally fully given of what's sometimes shared. Therefore, learn to forgive.

The enigma, Al Theroux.

Carolyn Chute
Writer

Well, I'm not going to call this advice. But I think it's an important thing a lot of people ought to try, no matter what their age. Have all your furniture be rocking chairs. Arrange them in a circle so that all the people who sit in your home have to face each other, look each other in the eye, and feel relaxed.

Another nice thing to try is forgetting everything you learned in public school. Especially the competition part—the "there are winners and losers" part. Try to think in terms of working together. EVERYBODY has an A+. It may not have been recognized in school. School recognizes only those things you can WIN at. Or the things you can do quietly at a desk. Everyone's A+ isn't visible or marketable or reflected in their possessions, appearance, or social graces.

Also remember that if something doesn't make sense to you, there's money and politics behind it.

Never ask "How are you today?" That is insincere unless you really want to hear the truth. I think we should all start saying "Cheerio!" again when we turn to leave.

Most world leaders are very bad people. We should all try to concentrate hard and turn them into soft little toads. If that doesn't work, at least don't revere them. Anyone who prances around smelling slightly of vinyl, who doesn't spend any time with honest people facing each other in creaky, comfy rocking chairs, who doesn't say "Cheerio!" upon departing from company isn't worth our esteem.

Paint your rocking chairs all different colors: pink, purple, yellow, mint, green, red, mauve, and two or three shades of blue.

Good luck. We'll be thinking about you.

Florence King
Writer

When I was getting ready to graduate from college in 1957, I was fed up and ready to drop from exhaustion, but still my mind kept telling me, "Hurry, hurry, hurry." I felt I had to *do* something, go on to the next step, whatever it was—career, graduate school, as long as it was important.

This is an American disease. Put yourself on cruise control and go into limbo for a year. I'm not talking about a neo-grand tour; don't bop around Europe, you'll just get in trouble. Nor am I talking about what your parents' generation called "dropping out." I mean forget about success for a while, get yourself an ordinary job, an ordinary place to live, and *live* without worrying about what Americans call, in uppercase, the Future.

Go somewhere different, but stay away from big cities. If you're from a place you call "godforsaken," go to a small city in another part of the country: Watertown, NY, Lexington, KY, Flagstaff, AZ, etc.

Get a dead-end job—they're plentiful now because nobody wants them. Tell your employer the truth: that you'll be around only a year or so, but promise to work hard. *Keep your promise.* Little triumphs are the pennies of self-esteem. If you do well in such a job and make yourself indispensable to somebody, you will realize Robert E. Lee's farewell words to his men after the surrender at Appomattox: "You will take with you the satisfaction that proceeds from a knowledge of duty faithfully performed."

Live alone, even at a financial sacrifice. If you have a roommate, the whole college uproar will just start all over again. Get a one-room apartment, or simply a room in the home of a nice widow. Get to know her. She's dying to tell somebody the story of her life, so listen.

Have a radio for emergency news, but no TV. Read, read, read. When you don't have to worry about passing exams on them, subjects you studied in school suddenly become interesting. Read my "desert island book," the one I'd want with me if I were shipwrecked: *The Prodigal Women* by Nancy Hale, a novel published in 1942. Girls will love it, and boys will learn more about women from it than anything I know of.

Stay chaste during your limbo year. Sex ruins reflection and self-knowledge; you're so busy analyzing the other person that you never get around to analyzing yourself.

What I am recommending is traditionally called "finding yourself." The difference is, there is no bohemian excess here, none of the "experiencing *everything*" that comprises nostalgia *de la boue*. It's productive, constructive goofing-off. The widow will remember you ever afterward as "that nice boy/girl who used to live here," and your employer will shake his head wonderingly and say, "By God, I wish I could find more like that!"

George Saunders
Writer

A Piece of Advice from an Old Fart, in the Form of
a Thought Experiment

Imagine the following scenario:

Two babies are born at precisely the same moment. Baby One
is healthy, with a great IQ and all its limbs and two kind, intelligent,
non-dysfunctional parents. Baby Two is sickly, not very bright, is
missing a limb or two, and is the child of two self-absorbed and stupid losers, one of whom has not been seen around lately and the
other of whom is a heroin addict. Now imagine this scenario
enacted a million times. Now imagine those two million babies
leaving the hospital and beginning to live their lives.

Statistically, the Baby Ones are going to have a better time of it
than the Baby Twos. Whatever random bad luck befalls the babies,
the Baby Ones will have more resources with which to engineer a
rebound. If a particular Baby One turns out to be, say, schizo-
phrenic, he or she will get better treatment than the corresponding
Baby Two, will be generally safer and better-cared-for, will more
likely have a stable home to return to. Having all his limbs, he can
go where he needs to go faster and easier. Ditto if Baby One is
depressed, or slow-witted, or wants to be an artist, or dreams of
having a family and supporting that family with dignity. A fortunate
birth, in other words, is a shock absorber.

Now we might ask ourselves: What did Baby One do to deserve
this fortunate birth? Or, conversely, what did Baby Two do to deserve
the unfortunate birth? Imagine the instant before birth. Even then, the
die is cast. Baby Two has done nothing, exerted no will, and yet the
missing limb is already missing, the slow brain already slow, the undesirable parents already undesirable. Now think back four months
before birth. Is the baby any more culpable? Six months before

birth? At the moment of conception? Is it possible to locate the moment when Baby Two's "culpability" begins?

Now consider a baby born with the particular neurological condition that will eventually cause him to manifest that suite of behaviors we call "paranoia." His life will be hell. Suspicious of everyone and everything, deeply anxious, he will have little pleasure, be able to forge no deep relationships. Now here is that baby fifteen seconds after conception. All the seeds of his future condition are present (otherwise, from what would it develop?). Is he "to blame"? What did he do, what choices did he make, that caused this condition in himself? Clearly, he "did" nothing to "deserve" his paranoia. If thirty years later, suspecting that his neighbor is spying on him, he trashes the neighbor's apartment and kills the neighbor's cat with a phone book, is he "to blame"? If so, at what point in his long life was he supposed to magically overcome/transcend his condition, and how?

Here, on the other hand, is a baby born with the particular neurological condition that will eventually cause him to manifest that suite of behaviors we call "being incredibly happy." His life will be heaven. Everything he touches will turn to gold. What doesn't turn to gold, he will use as fodder for contemplation, and will be the better for it. He will be able to love and trust people and get true pleasure from them. He is capable and self-assured, and acquires a huge fortune and performs a long list of truly good deeds. Now here is that baby fifteen seconds after conception. All the seeds of his condition are present (otherwise, from what would it develop?). Can he, justifiably (at fifteen seconds old), "take credit" for himself? What did he do, what choices did he make, that caused this condition of future happiness to manifest? Where was the moment of the exertion of will? Where was the decision? There was no exertion of will and no decision. There was only fulfillment of a pattern that began long before his conception. So if, thirty years later, in the company of his beautiful wife, whom he loves deeply, Baby One accepts the Nobel prize, then drives away in his Porsche, listening to Mozart, toward his gorgeous home, where his beloved children wait, thinking loving thoughts of him, can he justifiably "take credit" for any of this? I think not. You would not blame a banana for being the banana that it is. You would not expect it to have autocorrected its bent stem or willed itself into a brighter shade of yellow. Why is it, then, so natural for us to blame a person for being the person she is, to expect her to autocorrect her shrillness, say, or to will herself into being a perkier, more efficient person? I now hear a voice from the gallery, crying, "But I am not a banana! I have made myself what I am! What about tenacity and self-improvement and persisting in our efforts until our noble cause is won?" I contend that not only is our innate level of pluck, say, hardwired at birth, but also our ability to improve our level of pluck, as well as our ability to improve our ability to improve our level of pluck. All of these are ceded to us at the moment that sperm meets egg. Our life, colored by the particulars of our experience, scrolls out from there. Otherwise, what is it, exactly, that causes Person A, at age forty, to be plucky and Person B, also forty, to be decidedly non-plucky? Is it some failure of intention? And at what point, precisely, did that failure occur?

The upshot of all of this is not a passive moral relativism that finds itself incapable of action in the world. If you repeatedly come to my house and drive your truck over my chickens, I had better get you arrested or have your truck taken away or somehow ironclad or elevate my chickens. But I would contend that my ability to protect my chickens actually improves as I realize that your desire to flatten my chickens is organic and comes out of somewhere and is not unmotivated or even objectively evil. It is as undeniable to who you are, at that instant, as is your hair color. Which is not to say that it cannot be changed. It can be changed. It must be changed. But dropping the idea that your actions are Evil, and that you are Monstrous, I enter a new moral space in which the emphasis is on seeing with clarity, rather that judging; on acting in the most effective way (that is, the way that most radically and permanently protects my chickens), rather than on constructing and punishing a Monster.

So this is my advice: Think about the above. See if it makes any sense to you. Then, at the moment when someone cuts you off in traffic or breaks your heart or begins bombing your ancestral village, take action from this position, and I think you will find that, in the end, you will less often sully yourself with judgmentalism and anger and hatred, and be more able to live your life fully and compassionately—which, after all, is really the point.

A twentysomething George Saunders. That's him on the right.

Quentin Crisp
Playwright, philosopher, wit

Never imagine that happiness is out there; it is always in here.

Never try to be unlike other people; only strive to be more and more like yourself.

Never tell your mother anything; whatever you say will one day be used against you.

And NEVER work; in fact, before you do anything, always ask yourself one question,

"Can I possibly get out of this?"

Crispy Dream: Quentin wrote on the back of this photo, "Quentin Crisp, age 26." He was actually 32. *Angus McBean photograph © The Harvard Theatre Collection, The Houghton Library. Used with permission*

Mark Simpson
Writer

Get Shallow

No impersonator: The young, hearty Mark Simpson, circa 1986.

"Superficiality," Oscar Wilde once said, *après* I think rather than *avant* his long stay at the Hotel Reading Gaol, "is the greatest vice." And *she* should know.

Bitching aside, whether Wilde was offering us a warning or a recommendation I cannot say. But whatever his meaning, nowadays superficiality—or rather its successor, shallowness—is the greatest virtue, in a world without any. Hence Wilde's fashionability today, though the poor love is regularly disinterred and dragged around by common, shallow shits he wouldn't have shared a bordello with. Ironically, and inevitably, a world of triteness claims him as its crass Christ. *De Profundis* indeed.

Who can doubt the existence of Progress? Shallowness is so much more *democratic* than superficiality. To carry off superficiality you had to be a fully paid-up member of the aesthetic movement, a Lord of Language educated at the world's greatest university in its Golden Age. Oh, and you had to be a rather good, if overrated, playwright. There was also a paradox at the "gay" heart of Wilde's superficiality: It was profound and poignant. Perhaps this was why it was also implicit in the Dorian deal that you would ultimately pay a terrible price for your investment in appearances, your dalliance with surfaces (this, not arrogance, is the real reason why he didn't catch that boat-train to France).

In contrast, shallowness is within everyone's grasp. To pull it off requires little or no reading, no green carnations, no foppery, no feasting with panthers, and no nasty comeuppance, except that

103

you might get your own TV series. You don't even need a nice line in aphorisms or have a portrait stashed in your attic. All that is required is a few shaggy, recycled HBO one-liners and a subscription to the Abercrombie & Fitch catalog.

The world has been inherited not by Wilde, but by his nemesis boyfriend-user Bosie, the tantruming disco bunny manqué waiting impatiently for poppers and steps to be invented. Paradoxically, it was Bosie who was the real aristocrat and Wilde the real wannabe. But of course, only a gentleman can afford to not behave like a gentleman. . . . "Oh, he's talking about postmodernism," I hear some of you yawn at the back. No, *postmodernism* is a word that tries to render shallowness as a studied superficiality, but only succeeds in turning it into *cultural studies*.

A studied *shallowness* was, however, the lifetime achievement of another Englishman, Quentin Crisp—someone who initially made a career out of being mistaken for Wilde, but was in fact more of a downmarket, less beautiful Bosie. (However, after *The Naked Civil Servant* came out in the 1970s, he spent the rest of his life playing John Hurt's understudy.) Like Wilde he had a (wannabe) aristocratic idea of superficiality—an intense idleness as a reaction to bourgeois mores. Unlike Wilde, however, Quentin really believed this pose and never actually did anything—except be massively fascinated by Quentin. Quentin was the Miss Haversham of the twentieth century, who had deduced that there was no Great Dark Man, that he had been thoroughly stood up at the altar by his own romantic expectations, but instead of compromising with the vulgarity of modern life he decided simply to boycott it and spend his years looking down his powdered nose. Hence he moved to the United States and became the queen of an England that never existed. Now the world is full of queens, hetero and homo, who I wish had never existed.

This is why Mr. Crisp's death was such a shock, despite his advanced years: As a celebrated/celebrity anachronism, as a form of animated house dust, he was thought exempt from boring details such as mortality and was expected, in fact positively *required* to live forever. His shallowness, like that of all modern celebrities, was supposed to distance him and us from the dreary facts of life.

But with or without the benefit of Mr. Crisp's snacking aphorisms, the historical momentum of shallowness is as unstoppable as (d)evolution itself. The Stoned Age in the '60s was superseded by the Bronzed Age in the '70s and the Irony Age in the '80s. We are now living in the Silicone (Implant) Age, which began sometime circa *Baywatch* in the '90s and will probably last until the end of time or until the world's strategic reserves of china clay (the main ingredient of glossy magazines) are exhausted—whichever is the longer. Man's scaly, fish-eyed, legless ancestors took millennia to haul themselves out of the primordial oceans gasping and floundering onto the beach; if they'd only waited a few more millennia they could have held a nice barbie there with their scaly, fish-eyed, legless descendants.

So is shallowness superficiality for stupid people? Would that it were! Shallowness is often called "dumbing down," but this is a mistake. Dumb can be deep. It takes smarts—or at least *cynicism*—to be shallow. Perhaps this is why dumbing down is sometimes called "wising up." Shallowness is not stupidity, which can have its own kind of grace and virtue, but rather it is deliberate, chosen stupidity: obtuseness in mirrored wraparound sunglasses.

So, finally getting to the point, albeit somewhat late in the day—what exactly is my advice to the younger generation? Well, as you may have noticed, I'm something of a pessimist and so perhaps not the best person to ask about the future. And, to be honest, I'm just a tad bitter too. Though, naturally, I do take some solace from the thought that, whatever advice I give you, you'll probably end up bitter like me anyway.

Oh, I could give you some malicious advice (which is probably the only kind there is—certainly it's the only kind worth giving) and really fuck your careers up by advising you to avoid shallowness and steer for darker waters. But it would be rather pointless. People like me made sure of that back in the Irony Age with our post-punk indulgence in "alternative" culture and rebellion, later franchising our experiences to pay our mortgages. Today's "alternative culture" is the shallowest of all—literally (pierced) skin-deep. "Rebellion" is the tritest form of conformity. It accepts an invitation to meet Emperor George Bush II at the White House and has a tantrum because it's turned away for wearing jeans and sneakers. Yes, you can run around the center of Seattle smashing Gap store windows and protesting against "capitalism," but everyone's just waiting for you to launch your own clothes label called "Capitalism."

So what, as Lenin said, is to be done? Search me, Mary. I'm happy to shamelessly dodge *that* question by resorting to giving you some "sensible" advice: Surrender to the voices already whispering, nay shouting in your ears every time you turn on the TV or the radio, open a magazine, or go to a bar: "Get shallow. And if you're already shallow, get *shallower*." Of course, the advantages of shallowness don't really need to be explained, but such is the pedantic nature of "sensible" advice that I will spell it out in the form of one of those irritating, Crispian little lists you find everywhere these days:

Reasons to Be Shallow:

1. You'll be beautiful. Which also means these days that:

2. You'll be popular. Which also means that:

3. You'll be rich. Which also means that:

4. You'll get laid. Which also means that:

5. You won't have time to read books like this. Or in fact, any books that don't feature advice on how to get even more beautiful/popular/rich/laid.

As dear old Oscar himself once pronounced, "Only fools don't judge by appearances." Of course, when he made this statement it was, like many of his aphorisms, a wise, funny, shocking, and subversive paradox. Nowadays, it's federal law. In our time, not even Bosie — *especially* not Bosie—would shag that fat old loser poof.

Bret Lott
Writer

Words of advice have no choice but to be condescending. That is, the idea of *advice* connotes that the one giving it knows more about the way the world works than the one receiving it, when we are all of us stumbling pretty much blind. My parents did, your parents did. I do, you do. My children will, your children will. So set it straight in your head right now: You will stumble.

All that's left, then, is the perfect truth that we are all stumbling together, so the only word of "advice" I guess I'd want to give, if you'll forgive my posing as though I know what I'm talking about, is to *learn compassion.* Unlike clairvoyance or intuition or the ability to grow blond hair instead of brown, compassion is a learned trait, a behavior that incorporates others into our own consciousness: We are in this together. It's not something passed down at conception, not instilled in us at secret ceremonies. You learn it.

And, at the risk of alienating entire legions of readers here, even at the risk of letting my words escape finding publication in this collection, I now make the amazingly unhip following statement: I know no better way to learn compassion than to look at the life of Jesus Christ. There, I said it. Understand that I am not here to propose you send money to the newest Jim Bakker stand-in or vote for Jerry Falwell or attend the crystal cathedral nearest you: These are all sour symptoms, ugly trappings of mutant forms of compassion. Real compassion comes from living each day we have with the knowledge we are all of us lost, leaving us with the only real reaction we can have to all the ugliness the world has to dish out at us: Either we do for others what we would want done for ourselves, or we perish, never having known what joy and fruition our feeble lives are capable of finding.

I know: vague answer. Too simple. Things are more complicated than that.

True. No argument here. But I am only one voice, my words

only the ones I myself can muster. The sad truth is that I know how little I know of the world—know, in fact, nothing other that, were it not for the relationship I have with Christ, the world would surely have run me down by now. It's too big of a place for me to stand alone in front of, to be good to and to find good in it, without the example of Christ's love to lead me. Certainly I will never find the level of compassion he carried, and never will. But trying to learn that compassion is enough, all we need to carry us through to whatever tragic or wonderful surprise the world has in store.

Jeweled words: Brett Lott as a young, wise man.

Lynda Barry
Artist, novelist

My father had a reel-to-reel tape recorder that he kept in this sort of "den" of his in the basement, which was really just a corner by the washer. When I'd go down to hang out with him, sometimes he'd have me read something I wrote in school into the microphone to "save for the people of the future." He recorded radio shows, my mom yelling, my brother singing commercials from TV, our dog barking, and himself burping. He was the one who introduced me to the idea of documenting ordinary things. His tapes were tossed out eventually—it's a long sad story why—and much later I realized that I was one of the people of the future that he was talking about. I've been obsessed with the idea of recovering the past ever since.

A time capsule is a lot easier to make than you would think. You just get a cardboard box and write the year on the side in felt pen and start putting things into it. You should think of saving the things that are part of everyday life for you. Wrappers from your favorite things to eat, notes from your friends, a school picture, a recording of the radio station you listen to in the morning (including the voice of the DJ and all the commercials), a tape of your friends eating lunch, tapes of your family, the sounds of home and school, the more ordinary the better. A lot of times we tend to think it's the special events that should be recorded but it turns out to be the ordinary things that give us the most powerful feelings later on. Once a year it's a really good idea to take a picture of every wall of your bedroom, and a picture of every room in your house. Throw a copy of a *TV Guide* in the box. A mail-order catalog. A magazine you like. A piece of paper with your parents' handwriting on it. If you're the journal-keeping type, throw that in. If you're not, jot down a few things about your life now and then. Normal things. Unremarkable things. You get the picture. . . . And at the end of the year, tape the box shut and write the year it should be opened on the top. Address it as a present to yourself for your birthday twenty years from now. I swear to you, it will be the best present you will ever get.

R. U. Sirius
Writer

Don't Worry About Selling Out. Just Don't Buy In.

Loosely defined, I've been into the "counterculture" for thirty-four years. I've seen a lot of young wild things come and go. I've watched twentysomethings accuse any artist or dissident who earns a living of selling out, only to cynically take a high position on the corporate ladder a couple of years later. Often, they've adopted a conservative ideology shortly thereafter. So my first bit of advice is this: Remember what I just said. Check yourself. Are you going to be one of these?

Let's say a few words about so-called Generation X. Let me tell you what I've seen with my own eyes. I've seen young men and women whining about how the boomer generation failed to live up to its principles. I've seen these very same people turn around an instant later and jump both feet first into the big dot-com Ponzi scheme.

Let's talk about the baby boomers. They took it right up to the edge of political and cultural revolution. They backpedaled a bit more slowly. They became conventional liberals in the '70s. And then, by a majority, they voted for Ronald Reagan in 1980. Many returned to the old-time religions of their families. Did they return to conventional religiosity because they really believe that Jehovah created the universe in seven days, or that Jesus Christ rose from the dead? Are you kidding me? Does the Pope shit Eminem CDs? They returned to traditional values for comfort. They returned because they were too lazy to think clearly. They returned so their kids could "learn some values."

What value do they teach their kids? Follow the crowd. What value do they fail to teach their kids? Think for yourself.

So this is my final bit of advice. If you want to change things, or even just remain true to your authentic muse, pace yourself. It's easy to be a total freak when you're young, but it's a lot cooler to be able to talk human to family members. If you don't get all more-radical-than-thou and too-hip-to-breathe now, you will feel less compelled to flip 180 degrees in the other direction when you finally confront your own weaknesses. If you need a job, get one. If you can get an interesting one, cool. If you must do something detestable, that's okay. Just don't believe in it.

Don't worry too much about selling out. Just don't buy in. As long as you don't buy in, your head will always be in the right place for further change and experimentation.

Charles Baxter
Writer

Rilke, in *The Notebooks of Malte Laurids Brigge*, invents a disease—a purely speculative disease—whose only identifying feature is that it takes on the characteristics of the person who has it. Although Rilke does not get down to cases, I think he means, or is talking about, people who are careful and who sicken and die of their carefulness; or oth-

Harmony in the world: Storyteller Charles Baxter.

ers who are generous and gradually get sick with that; or anyone whose virtues walk through a mirror and come back as vices, looking the same, but dominant. Another word for this process is piety, in its negative sense. You get pious about what you believe in, and soon you become a grotesque embodiment of that belief.

This morning I have been thinking about speed, and how pious early twenty-first century culture has become about it. AT&T is now running television commercials that promise to save you three seconds of time in reaching your caller. The myth of speed is connected to the myth of productivity, and both of these myths are, I think, making people crazy. It's as if we are under instructions to consume things, as much as we can, and to do it in a hurry. To say that a movie or a book is "slow" is now understood to be a criticism. But love is usually slow; tenderness is always slow; understanding comes in slow stages. Valuing the earth, and others, takes time. Any kind of intelligent humanism and ecology must fight the ideology of speed. The quick fuck is the enemy of slow lovemaking; the tree outside my window took forty years to reach its current size; and boredom may just be the last stage before complete enlightenment.

We must produce less, consume less, and do everything more slowly. We must grow to love whatever happens slowly. Productivity for its own sake must be resisted. We should emulate the elephant.

Anita O'Day
Singer

Just get up there and let it rip!

Tom Robbins
Writer

At least once a day, stand before a mirror and repeat after me: "I'm not a Buick, I'm a Buddha!"

At least once a week, renew a solemn vow to limit consumption and restrict procreation.

At least once a month, remind yourself that your purpose on earth is to enlarge your soul, light up your brain, and liberate your spirit.

At least once a year, go out and sleep where the bears sleep.

Thus, having gotten mind and body in order, and having learned not to take yourself too seriously, you are free to climb aboard that strange torpedo and ride it to wherever it's going.

A sprightly Tom Robbins bob, bob, bobbin' along.

Ian Shoales
Writer

When I was a young person, the only advice I ever got was from my high school vocational adviser. He had a file folder full of test results (aptitude, psychology, attitude, etc.) that indicated that I should seek a career in the social sciences.

There's no such occupation anymore, of course. The "social scientist" has been replaced by the "grief counselor." But even at the time, I couldn't bring myself to embrace this career choice.

For one thing, a social scientist always wore a white nylon shirt, something I could not in good conscience do. For another, the job of the social scientist was to generate data, which were either manipulated by politicians to justify an action they were going to do anyway, or used by high school vocational advisers so they could offer advice to people like me who wouldn't take it anyway.

It was a vicious cycle, and I did my best to help break it.

Instead of a social scientist, I became a social gadfly. It doesn't pay well, but at least I don't have to wear nylon shirts. And I don't have to use words like "socioeconomic" or "dysfunctional" unless I feel like it. Best of all, I don't have to give advice.

What I do is emit strangled cries of rage, delivered in a fast-paced nasal whine, dripping with sarcasm and snide self-loathing. It's hard to fit advice into that. Also, you need a crinkly smile to dispense advice, like Ronald Reagan's or Ward Cleaver's. I don't crinkle. I seethe.

Let's say that I invited a young person to sit on ol' Ian's knee to listen to my words of wisdom. People would see the young person perched on my knee and think I was either a Dutch uncle or a pervert. My tenuous livelihood as gadfly would not survive either interpretation.

Do young people even need my advice? Well, who is the young person of today? I know you like to play violent computer games in cubicles lit by fluorescent lights. Okay. Whatever. You read Stephen

King novels as fast as he can write them. I suspect you'd like to be reading one right this minute, instead of listening to my advice. Go ahead. Read as many Stephen King novels as you can get your hands on. Maybe something will rub off on you, and you too can make millions grossing out young people with thick novels badly in need of an editor. Perhaps one of them might even be turned into a violent computer game. Cool! I'm "down" with that.

Perhaps you enjoy the overproduced recordings of morose yet energetic boy bands, whose singers all sound like they're fighting a cold. I can relate to that as well. I was morose myself as a youngster. I'd dress in black and stand on the fringes of parties, hoping a girl even more sullen than myself would notice me, at which point we would alternate between bursts of sneering at others and wild sexual activity. This never happened for me, frankly, but it might work for you. Again, I say, "Go ahead!" Indulge in wild sexual activity (with protection, of course), preferably with another person, but go easy on the sullen part. There's time enough for sulky bitterness when you reach my age. At my age, you'll need all the self-pity you can muster. Don't squander it while you're young.

I also know that you enjoy watching movies in which other young people get hacked to bits by a maniac. I don't know how you can spend your parents' good money on this, but then again, when I was a tad, the movies I frequented featured French actresses taking their shirts off while spouting long Marxist monologues directly into the camera. Ask me today which I'd rather see, a movie about dismembered teenagers, or a movie about semi-clad Marxists, and, well, it's pretty much a toss-up. So, I'll crinkle my face into a smile (ow! that hurts!) and say, "Go see whatever movie you want, kids!" Except Tom Cruise movies.

"Who the hell are you to give advice?" I hear you ask. I happen to be a guy who met the actor who played Freddie Krueger, in a bar in Santa Monica. He seemed like a nice guy, and was happy to be working steadily. I'm also a guy who saw Dr. Ruth once, across a crowded theater lobby in downtown Manhattan. Man, was she short!

So I'm a guy who's met or seen the great or near great. Ted Koppel even cadged a cigarette from me once, back when I was smoking. I've traveled the country as restlessly as Jack Kerouac, or an entrepreneur with terminal jet lag.

Therefore—and take this with a grain of salt as big as Lot's wife—I urge you to hate as many things as possible. I'm not just talking about the obvious targets of hatred—like mimes, every third stand-up comic, ludicrous dot-com businesses, commercials, television, American foreign policy, and Tom Cruise movies—I'm talking about things that strike even closer to home, like checks from your mom (hate them, but cash them) and people who use the words "empower" or "adjudicate" in everyday conversation. Hate any group that organizes for a purpose—football leagues, baseball teams, political parties, costume parties, diplomatic corps, religions, unions, corporations, and the social sciences, to name a few examples.

Remember always, however, that your hatred won't change anything. Foreign policy will continue, despite your opinion. *The Washington Post* will keep on publishing, no matter what conservatives write about it. The objects of our scorn will remain, irresistible, immovable, and immune from your hatred. Your hatred is there for you and you alone.

To paraphrase what the hippies used to say (and don't you hate hippies, though?), "Let your hatred go. If it's yours, it will come back to you. If it doesn't come back, it was never yours to begin with." While waiting to see what your hatred does, go ahead, have some wild sexual activity. Tell them Ian sent you! Now get off the knee, kid.

C. D. Payne
Writer

Things to do before you're twenty:

Resist the urge to transfer to a military academy unless your probation officer insists.

Make passionate love in your parents' bed (but do exclude your parents).

Spend a long, wild weekend in New York City. (If you're a NYC native, take a bus to Camden, New Jersey, for perspective.)

Elope with your childhood sweetheart.

Do not rest until someone calls you "trailer trash" to your face.

Learn to type. It's always nice to have at least one marketable skill that doesn't involve a shovel or a spatula.

Enroll in a college at least two hundred miles from home (far enough away to discourage parental visits, but still affordable for shipping home your laundry).

Things to do before you're twenty-five:

Resist the impulse to go to law school. If you must sell out for big bucks, go to work for a tobacco company instead.

Learn to cook. People who eat only in restaurants eventually have to go through doors sideways.

Buy a car that seats no more than two and sports a non-rigid top (Geo Metros and Cushmans don't count).

Divorce your childhood sweetheart.

Resist the impulse to start saving for retirement.

Make love with someone of the same sex to see if you're missing anything. If you're gay, try it with the opposite sex.

Ask for a raise without worrying if your employer can afford it (after all, they're not worrying if you can live on what they pay you).

Go abroad for two weeks every year. If you reside in the Midwest, make it three weeks. (No, Tijuana doesn't count.)

Move out of your parents' house—if only to improve your slim chance of having a normal sex life.

Things to do before you're thirty:

Inform your boss that he or she would have to undergo significant personal growth to achieve emotional parity with a cockroach.

Put down the remote and pick up a book. Read some history. It's always nice to know which came first: the Civil War or the Studebaker Lark.

Get remarried in Las Vegas—ignoring your friends' comments that your new love seems remarkably similar to your previous spouse.

Try to cultivate an appreciation for contemporary popular music. Failing that, become a rabid fan of Frank Sinatra.

Develop outside interests, such as a hobby not involving Barbie dolls, high explosives, complex fishing tackle, or secret rituals entailing elaborate handshakes.

Have a child, or, better yet, adopt a cat.

Buy a house, even though the monthly payments will suck up 87 percent of your disposable income.

Become dissatisfied with life, quit your job, sell all your possessions, ride around the world on a moped to acquire wisdom, broaden your horizons, and stumble upon a fabulous business idea that will net you millions, rocket you into the good life, and lead to premature artery hardening with fatal consequences at age forty-two.

Revolting youth:
Novelist C. D. Payne.

C. D. Payne

Bruce Benderson
Writer, translator

Take my advice. What an obnoxious imperative! Never once as a young man did I listen to it. Advice coming from mouths fighting gum disease and brains fighting regret? In other words, from a different physiological reality. Take their advice? And trade my resilience, energy, thirst for adventure, and inability to imagine death for their fragility, fatigue, need for security, and nearness to the grave? Never!

Yet the advice-givers were right nine times out of ten. Sex with strangers is mucho risky, drugs can destroy brain cells, friends can become users, an artist's career is a gamble full of frustrations, old age sucks without money. But maybe old age just sucks.

No, I didn't take their advice and . . . I think have been lucky. I've slalomed through the heady experiments of sex, the heartbreaks of love and the bitterness of lost friendships, the toxic experiments of drug-taking, and the bohemia of no money and have pulled from them a rich fantasy life, and perhaps even some hyperawareness of the Other. And maybe my excursions into the libidinal realities of other ages, races, and classes, mostly by fucking, has all been narcissistic, but it makes stunning copy! It has made me a better writer, perhaps a more compassionate writer. And yes, I could have died.

P is twenty and already has a completed novel and a music CD under his belt. He told me that he has to become famous—soon—because he lacks interpersonal skills, and getting attention that way is the only way to feel that he exists. Take my advice, P (*Did I say that?*): If success is what you're looking for, get an MBA. But if you want pleasure, then think of your art as play. Art is the radical decision to enjoy yourself at all cost. And serious pleasure, despite what they tell you, can engender meaning, creativity. Which doesn't mean that an artist doesn't work his ass off. It only means that in striving to rework the world according to one's fantasies, for the purpose of pleasure, beauty, and the kink-filled shock of having stumbled upon original meaning, the need for fame should play a miniscule part.

So take my advice. Just don't blame me if you fuck up.

The truth is out there: Bruce Benderson, no pretender.

W. V. Quine
Philosopher

Cultivate the inquiring mind. Don't suppress a question, however trivial, that sparks your curiosity. Track it down or look it up as soon as you can.

Enjoy what you are doing, what you are seeing, as fully as you can find anything in it to enjoy. Savor the moment, the scene, the sound, the word. *Carpe diem, horam, minutam.*

Try for a career where you can take pleasure or satisfaction in your work rather than just in the leisure after work. Earning less but enjoying your work, you are getting good returns for the sacrificed difference in income.

You must face dull chores and discipline too, for a rewarding expertise takes a dull deal of training. What is wanted is shrewd cost-accounting and a prudent but not excessive investment in futures.

Above all, cultivate easy and sincere friendships with kindred spirits and enter into them with generous sympathy. Sharing is the sovereign lubricant against the harshness of life.

Mark Helprin
Writer

First, don't look at television. Television makes people stupid. Second, don't take drugs. Drugs make people stupid. Third, read two newspapers of opposing tendencies. If you don't, you can't make informed political judgments. Fourth, don't run in packs. Fifth, get as much higher education as you can, and then leave. At the time of this writing, universities are fulfilling a mission once entrusted to insane asylums. A sojourn in academe may be refreshing, but as soon as you begin to get inert, get out. Sixth, don't get killed. You may not know this, or, more correctly, you may not feel it, but, after you get killed you don't come back. A lot of my friends are no longer with us. People don't think of them day and night, so it probably would have been better for them to have stuck around a little longer. Seventh, don't be self-centered. The world is much bigger and much more interesting than you are. If you spend your time thinking about yourself, you forego most of what exists. Eighth, realize that cars are ugly. That's the first step in understanding what is beautiful. Ninth, don't eat dead animals that you find by the side of the road. Tenth, remember that your metabolism will age and your joints will stiffen too, so don't laugh at old people who do funny exercises. Finally, understand that time is passing very slowly for you now. Things are more languid and smooth than they will ever be, no matter how much success you have in the future. Take advantage of it. Remember it.

Scott Russell Sanders
Writer

At the time I write these words, my son is twelve years old and my daughter is seventeen. I love them with the bewildering devotion that fathers and mothers have been feeling toward their children for thousands of generations. Perhaps my love and care can help them toward a decent marriage and a worthy career; perhaps I can even help them find a humane community in which to live; but nothing I do can assure them of a peaceful country or an unspoiled planet. My generation has passed on to theirs a diminished legacy— an earth that is more violent, more crowded, more polluted, less fertile, and less humane than the one onto which we were born. Nothing that we have achieved in science or technology or art can make up for the squandering of this inheritance.

When I offer advice to my children and their generation, therefore, I do so with humility. I do so knowing that we have burdened them with terrible dangers and debts. These are words I have tried to live by, words I give to them: Love the land and all that grows on it. Remember that the earth, with its manifold life, is primary, and we are secondary. The earth preceded us and will outlast us. Our planet is not a spaceship, with us at the controls; it is more like a house, in which we are guests. The earth has made us possible, and moment by moment it sustains us. We are not set apart, not superior, not a chosen species; we are made from the earth, of the earth, earthy. Love simply. By that I mean, think about what you actually need for a good life, not what friends or ads have taught you to want. Don't let television or magazines dictate your desires, and don't let Hollywood manufacture your dreams. You are *not* what you own. Do not measure yourself or others by the yardstick of money. Live in such a way that others, also, may have what they need.

Make peace. Seek understanding and show respect in your personal relations. At work and in your community, help take away the causes of strife, including poverty, racism, and the exploitation of person by person.

When I say these things, I do not mean for you to shoulder the burdens of the world. Do what is possible within the reach of your voice and hands; trust that others elsewhere are also doing their part.

Find a person to love who enlarges the world for you, and find a place to live that nourishes you; and then commit yourself to that person and that place.

Listen to your heart, but not so intently that you fail to notice what those around you are feeling.

Your mind is your greatest gift—all of your mind, the power of dreaming and reasoning, intellect and imagination. Use this gift with delight and gratitude. Through your mind you may sense the greater power that creates and sustains all things.

Learn from others, but think for yourself. Read books, the best of those written in your own time, along with those that thoughtful people in other ages have considered valuable.

Treasure your questions; don't stop asking them simply because the answers are hard to find. In particular, don't stop asking those questions that the world's religions have traditionally sought to answer. To understand as well as we can who we truly are and in what sort of world we have been set down may be our most important task.

Be joyful. Sing and dance. Relish the beauty that is in the world and the beauty that humans are capable of making together. Take pleasure in music, in art and language; take pleasure in food, in the body's motion. Be thankful for the gift of life, your own and that of all other creatures. Preserve your sense that existence itself is miraculous, and that the world, for all its wounds, is rich beyond our deserving or reckoning.

Scott Russell Sanders

Eileen Myles
Poet

Survival of a Starfish

I suppose in retrospect the only people who were important to me when I was young were the people who saw me and these people generally told me that I was a lesbian and a drunk. Actually I'm thinking of one person in particular who had

Cool for us: Absolute Eileen Myles.

these two distinct and shocking takes on me and naturally it was pretty disturbing, but I also felt captured, *seen* inside out in some fashion, and I think all of us need to be some kind of starfish to survive—have to be able to put our insides out and vice versa in order to keep our balance in the world. So it helps to encounter people who can see what you are secretly worrying about or even *doing* and maybe not so much reassure you about these things—'cause really there's no good news about alcohol and lesbianism, unlike say Christianity, a font from which there is always good news, but booze and lesbianism—well if you are thinking about these things you would do well just to drink a lot unabashedly and see where *that* goes and likewise be encouraged to realize that being a lesbian is nothing more than being a woman who wants to explore being female in a deep and profound way and by and large that will always be a big mistake in "our" culture—I mean the larger culture, if you need to think of that as that, though, frankly, I think the larger thing is a place where all the little things get erased, and I think that being female in any way that isn't about putting cheese on a woman and melting the cheese and then serving her on a bun, but being female in a way that has to do with how it feels to be female now, for me at fifty-one or you at twenty-three or twenty-nine, is still a pretty radical position because women are supposed to be of use—to men, not ever to each other—so you can see the difficulty of lesbianism, of wanting to be female, about being female, and worse maybe wanting to have sex with one like yourself.

Like, think about a female masturbating. Who is that for? I think as an image it's for men. I'm thinking about a girl in her twenties masturbating. Why not? But is that hers, that moment? It's got to be, right? Everything else in the world depends upon that being her act, not anyone else's, but everything in the world says that that moment is worth so much money, it should be sold, it shouldn't be hers alone. Maybe she should do it with another girl, a girl in her twenties. Is it theirs, that act of them masturbating, or even having sex together? Are those great bodies theirs, or the culture's? Are they allowed to do this alone? How about a boy mastur-

This is what Girl Scouts should be doing.
Little girls whispering to each other,
we're dangerous, we're dangerous.

bating, a boy in his twenties. Is it his experience? I think so. He's coming of age, isn't he? The girl is not doing that, she's doing something different. If she decides to not be of use, it's dangerous. The culture will tell her she's in danger, but really the opposite is true. She's *dangerous*. Every female who decides not to go along with the necessity for all the most important parts of her life, all those great private parts, being forked over to the culture for use—she is in deep shit now and really ought to know it, but maybe she ought to know for a moment that the culture is threatened by her, that's *the problem*. It's a secret. She ought to tell it to another girl, a whole lot of girls. This is what Girl Scouts should be doing. Little girls whispering to each other, *we're dangerous, we're dangerous.* Now I don't think there's anything wrong with girls getting drunk except in the sense that one can become prey when she gets too juiced—she can stray away from her gang of drunken women and boom, next thing you know she gets raped. This is actually true. Women alone become prey for men. There's kind of a war out there—they'll be slapping the cheese and the toasted bun on you real fast. In my own personal life I prefer to be sober. I feel more dangerous this way, as a lesbian, and I like it. But you know I'd also just like to add that being a lesbian is not the only way for women to go. I'm really interested in this issue of female strength, girls whispering, shouting, and swaggering through the world, protecting their own interests, turning their insides out, seeing what they like about the world, bringing that in. A girl might want a man, I say good luck to her—I don't know much about that, I have not practiced those ways in years—but mainly I want to say the girl should get her strength from her primary relationship—with a network of loud, subtle, tomboyish, feminine, versatile, some lesbian, some possibly heterosexual, some even wanting to have children—whatever, and I say to that kind of women, *I* turn my back on those kind of experiences, but I don't advocate that all women should. I just think starting maybe from the primacy of a girl masturbating, possibly alone, possibly with her friend and becoming dangerous from there, I advocate that kind of power—and also all aspects of her friendship with other girls. And also, that girl should write.

Maybe I'll just talk about *that* aspect for a moment. The writing. See, the person who told me I was a dyke and an alcoholic was a man. A fag, he's dead now, died of AIDS. Paul Johnson was his name. He lived in Massachusetts, I met him in college. But what if I didn't meet Paul? Maybe I could have read it in a book. Now of course the books of our culture tell girls how to be girls-of-use. The books that tell us how to be dangerous and different are only being written now. They have always been written, but they have not always been printed; sometimes they have and they have gone out of print, but most importantly in our time we have to write those books and pass on this message of the great vast female inside, the mind inside the mysterious female body, the dreaming female consciousness that is trying to wake up; we should pass that message on. That's what we have to do today; that's what I just did. Otherwise we will only live and die. We have to change things. We have to get our insides out. And women can take that in. Later on I would like to help men. But women first.

John Shirley
Writer

It's all about mastering the paradox. And here's the paradox: It's possible to fully commit, to go all the way, to go to (sometimes) extremes, to play the Jimi Hendrix guitar solo, to get deeply involved in a new enterprise, to get into demanding experiments with your life, to ski down the steepest mountainside, to be all-out in whatever you do—and yet, all the time, to be centered, skeptical, balanced, compassionate.

Balanced is important; and that balance, in even the most extreme situations, is achieved by a kind of open-minded skepticism and by a certain level of pure consciousness.

Just entertain these hypothetical questions for a moment: What if we're a lot more unconscious than we know? What if, even when we think we've got everything worked out and planned out, we're actually, in certain ways, just reacting to things? What if we don't make conscious choices—even when we think we're making conscious choices? What if we're more asleep than we realize, even as we function acceptably in our waking day? What if it were possible to be a little more awake, a little more conscious, so that you can do what you really want to do—so that you can find out what that is—and so that you're not just blundering along from one thing to the next in life?

For example, how many times do you hear about people who go into a career, put twenty-five years into it, and then say, "It seemed like a good idea at time. . . . But if I had to do it over again . . ."

So how can we get to the place where we don't have to wish we had it to do over again—where we stand a better chance of being able to do it right the first time?

On the one hand, we have to accept what arises in our lives with dignity and just plain coolness, or we become floundering and ridiculous; on the other hand, it is possible to be aware of where we're going at a higher level than the "default" level we're usually in, so we can make more conscious choices. If you have to walk along a dark mountain path, don't you prefer to have a flashlight to shine on the path ahead? I would suggest that it is possible to have that flashlight in life all the time. What does a flashlight give us? *Light.*

That is, a flashlight *sheds light.* It is like the faculty of attention—if we turn our full attention to something, we learn more about that thing. We are seeing it with more light. Our *attention* is our "flashlight." So it's all about how much and how fine an attention we consciously bring to life. This quality of attention doesn't make us hesitant, or slow to decide, particularly—just as the flashlight doesn't make us hang back on the trail. So, how do we get to this better quality of attention? With attention! That is, we turn our attention *on* our attention; we start by trying to see how we don't pay attention. We sort of keep that flashlight *on ourselves.* "Know thyself" has been an honored ancient teaching, and it's still a cornerstone of the world's greatest philosophies. If you watch yourself honestly, in a detached way—not guilt-tripping yourself when you screw up—you gradually learn where it was that you were just blundering along, reacting sort of mechanically, and being asleep even as you were in your waking day. Another way to make this happen is by returning your whole attention to the present—to what's happening *now,* in *this moment,* and *this* moment, and on—within yourself and around you.

"The present is the place where Time touches eternity," C. S. Lewis once said. By turning your attention to the present, you can touch eternity, and that gives you a kind of cosmic perspective on yourself. By degrees, we get a little more aware, a little more conscious—just a little more all the time, as we make these small, continuing efforts. And inevitably we will find that we get more out of the process than just being able to make better choices; we get a possibility of opening up to something higher than ourselves, of understanding something of why we're here in the world in the first place, and who we really are.

There's a kind of meditation, found in various traditions of self-knowledge (like Dzogchen Buddhism, Zen, the Gurdjieff Foundation, Sufism, Thomas Keating's contemplative methods, and in other places), that enhances our ability to be present, to be a little more aware. These teachings give us a certain balance, a certain skepticism, and a little more wakeful awareness that enable us to choose where to commit ourselves intelligently, and to be the best people we can be. They help guide us along even those highly energized extremities . . . shedding a little light on an otherwise shadowy path.

Abbie Hoffman
American dissident

Don't piss on the shoe of someone standing behind you.

Don't give blind faith or allegiance to any authority simply because it's been officially designated.

As quickly as you can in life deal with your fear of death, the rest—scorn of the family, community, authority, critics of all sorts, fear of being embarrassed because your ideas and actions are ill-mannered—will all appear secondary after you conquer this rather stubborn anxiety.

Hope for the best and prepare for the worst—remembering the words of Jose Ortega Y Gasset: "Life happens while you're busy making plans."

When your inner conscience strongly conflicts with desires for money and security, go with your conscience.

Be prepared to be lonely in life but always willing to fuck 'em if they can't take a joke.

In other words, when all is said and done, don't lose your sense of humor.

Dr. Laura Schlessinger
Author, radio host

My first reaction to this project—giving advice to young people—is to wonder when I got old enough to be asked to contribute to such an endeavor. Why, just yesterday I dyed the gray right outta my hair! Actually, even with that bit of ego-glitch, I am honored that I have been tapped as a worthy resource for you.

And perhaps, that is my first lesson for you; it is a natural part of youth to see the world as a kind of snapshot, static and permanent. You will always be young. Right? Nothing you do now can possibly be a problem for you later on—because "later on" is a time you can't see in that snapshot. This is especially true if you don't come from an intact, multigenerational family experience. While extended families sometimes can be a pain or an embarrassment, at least they give you the experience of all the seasons of life, and with that, a recognition that what you do today is not only a part of the world's history (no small burden), but also an inexorable part of your own future (no small threat).

Therefore, in spite of temptations and frustrations, in spite of desires and imagined needs, in spite of impulse and opportunity, in spite of yourself, make choices and behave as though the camera crews of the future were already filming your retrospective. Believe it or not, it all comes back to bite you—even those things you imagine no one will ever discover.

My second piece of advice is somewhat related to protecting your lifetime scorecard: Never sell your soul. One usually thinks of soul-selling in grand terms, like grand larceny or cheating on your income tax. But that's usually not how soul-selling goes. There is an element of Jewish law related to stealing. It forbids even taking a splinter off someone's wood fence. A splinter? Aw, come on! But think about it. If each day you take just one thin splinter, eventually the fence will fall. Don't sell even tiny pieces of your soul, because the same thing will happen to you.

Many times you will justify cutting that small corner, taking a small edge, telling a small lie (and I don't include white lies to preserve someone's feelings) for personal gain, or doing what you know isn't right because it will allow you to do some good . . . eventually. I remember one colleague of mine with a TV show who admits to doing tasteless things, rationalizing that this would get him ratings; ratings would keep him on the air; and if he stayed on the air, he would be able to do important work. Wrong. When you do less than your best with any aspect of your life, you lose the respect and trust of others, momentum toward your virtuous goals, your will to persevere against evil, and finally, the opportunity to do the good. It's frightening how easily bad habits are formed from such splinters of rationalization.

Let's tally. Number one: Live your life so that in twenty years you can look back on yourself with minimum regret and shame, and maximum respect. Number two: Never sell even slivers of your soul. My next lesson is very countercultural. It's about balance. Everything I read about modern life refers to the difficulties of balancing work, spouse, children, family, community responsibilities, health, spirituality, hobbies, and relaxation. Clearly, the inference is we're supposed to be doing all of these things . . . simultaneously. Truth be told, it's not possible. In trying to do everything, to have everything, it's generally the most important aspects that end up being leftovers:

A doc to watch out for: Vintage Laura Schlessinger.

children, marriage, and a relationship with G-d (which puts all of life in perspective and gives it ultimate meaning and purpose).

Forget balance. Think choices. You must order your priorities, and only do what you can do well. You can't do well as a parent when your kid is in full-time day care. Ask yourself, could you be a good employee if you had a surrogate show up to work for you every day? You can't do well as a spouse when you're rarely even home for dinner; you won't do well as a human being when your spiritual life is confined to religious holiday dinners.

I am heartened by the thousands of people who have written me over the last few years, joyous and fulfilled after accepting the simple truth that life is not about personal aggrandizement, acquisition, and self-fulfillment. In other words, man cannot live by "me, me, me" alone. I don't wonder that so many people search blindly for the "meaning of life." What they don't seem to understand is that life does not have meaning through mere existence or acquisition or fun. The meaning of life is inherent in the connections we make to others through honor and obligation. I have shaped my career to my family life—not the other way around. It is amazing that I have achieved success doing so, but that just proves it's doable. It's the will that's often missing. The motivation to give, to fulfill obligations, and to sacrifice has been replaced by the demand for personal rights, for acquisition and perpetual fulfillment. With that attitude, what you have—and are—ultimately will be unsatisfying. Live for something and someone. That's what makes you important.

Tally update. Number one: Live your life so that in twenty years you can look back with minimum regret and shame, and maximum respect. Number two: Never sell even slivers of your soul. Number three: Forget balance. Life requires honorable choices. Next, be courageous about and true to your mission. I believe that each of us has been anointed by G-d with a mission, some purpose that is our unique contribution to perfecting the world. G-d made the earth, the sun, the water, the soil, and all of life. It takes human beings to plant the seeds, harvest the grain, and bake the bread. Human beings and G-d are like a team. We need each other to play out the game.

Your role is to find out what your purpose is, and to face it with nobility, integrity, and courage. As in any game, there are always the opposing players, determined to keep you from that noble goal—your mission. You may become deflated or afraid, but find a way past those emotions, and stay true to your mission. So many people count on you; usually more than you'll ever know.

Finally, it is easy to dismiss G-d and religion. After all, there is so much that is difficult to understand, and some things that are so hard to accept. I'd like to leave you with two thoughts about the G-d question. First, without G-d, there is no universal morality and no eternal justice. Second, without G-d, you really are trapped in that static snapshot, with no meaning to life beyond turf, breeding, eating, and survival. Is that really a better scenario?

Even if you're struggling with G-d—and heaven knows I do—why don't you live as though G-d were a fact. I believe it will lead you down better paths with better people.

P.S.: When you slip up, be seriously remorseful, accept responsibility, do what you can to repair what you've done, and make sure you don't repeat it. Then, forgive and get back to your mission—the universe is counting on it!

Final tally:

Live your life so that in twenty years you can look back with minimum regret.

Never sell even slivers of your soul.

Forget balance. Have the integrity to make honorable choices.

Find and face your mission with courage.

Live in G-dliness.

Be willing to repent (remorse, responsibility, reparations, no repetition).

Bruce LaBruce
Filmmaker, writer

The Love God?; or, How to Succeed in Pornography without Really Trying—A Cautionary Tale

In *The Love God?*, a rather unjustly maligned Don Knotts vehicle from 1969, Abner Peacock, a nerdy, nebishy ornithologist played by Knotts himself, is hoodwinked by various lawyers and generic Mafioso types into transforming his modest bird-watching magazine into an international *Playboy*-like porno publication called *Peacock*, with Abner himself reluctantly transformed into the pajama-wearing sex-god figurehead à la Hugh Hefner. This is the apotheosis of Knotts, who had his first big success in the early '60s as Barney Fife, the bug-eyed, nervous deputy on *The Andy Griffith Show*, but who, by the end of the decade, had become an unlikely sex symbol.

A series of starring vehicles for Knotts, with his goldfish face and an Adam's apple the size of a small fist, posited him as the ninety-eight-pound weakling constantly thrown into circumstances in which he had to prove his manhood. In *The Reluctant Astronaut* (a title I borrowed from for my premature memoirs, *The Reluctant Pornographer*), he plays a childlike carnival ride operator terrified of heights who becomes an unwilling astronaut. In *The Shakiest Gun in the West*, he is a meek dentist propped up as a macho gunslinger by a sexy, conniving woman with whom he is involved in a sham marriage, his "shaky gun" cleverly signifying a limp dick. (To add to the ambiguity, his dentist character has moved to the Wild West "to fight oral ignorance," which may provide a clue to the impotent Knotts's hidden sexual allure.)

But it's in *The Love God?* that all the sexual ambivalence and homosexual panic that is at the heart of the Knotts image is deliriously articulated. While the skinny, innocent Abner sits in court for an obscenity trial, the public defender rails that it's his duty to protect the public from "the smut and moral corruption spewed forth like garbage from the lecherous, vile, lewd, and licentious mind of this filthy little degenerate." As Abner squirms, he continues: "Look at his face—it's the face of a smut-monger. Look at his body— thin, wasted away by the dissipation and debauchery of a life of unspeakable orgies and depravity." (A pre-AIDS reference, Knotts nevertheless was always coded as frail, sickly, and thus, homosexual.) "The Marquis de Sade would have considered him a peer in his search for lechery," he finishes triumphantly. With such a buildup, the women in the courtroom and all over America become aroused by Peacock, including Liza LaMonica, the cynical, ambitious maga- zine editor who transforms him into a sexual icon. Despite, or per- haps owing to, his sexual shortcomings, Don Knotts always ended up attracting a sexy girl.

Enter LaBruce. Like Knotts, whose characters invariably came from a working class, rural, or small-town environment, I was a fey, freckled farmboy who came to Toronto in the early '80s to attend film school. Although I started out in film production, moviemak- ing was too expensive and too technical for me (technophobia was yet another of my unmasculine traits), so I went into the more bookish field of film theory instead. As a homosexual virgin in my early twenties, I attempted to penetrate the gay scene, but found it alienating—superficial and conformist. By this time, homosexuals had strayed from their early roots of distinct individual style and flamboyance—which exerted itself as an invisible influence on fashion, art, and culture—and moved toward a more uniform aes- thetic, clonelike and vaguely fascist. (It's no accident that the clone look would, by the '90s, evolve literally, particularly in Europe, into a neo-Nazi skinhead bootboy look.) Politically, the gay movement was already moving in a more assimilationist direction: The desire to be accepted and treated like everyone else was predicated on a more conservative approach, which also meant distancing itself from its more extreme and radical elements.

Whereas the original agenda of gay activism had been based on notions of sexual liberation, antiauthoritarian behavior, and the expression of difference, by the mid-'80s the order of the day was conformity, fitting in, and fixing identity as nonthreatening in order for it to become palatable to the masses. This could be partly attributed to the advent of the AIDS, which reduced the gay movement to a narrow set of political imperatives in service of a "health crisis." (That this crisis could be directly attributed to extreme sexual promiscuity and the misuse of antibiotics to treat venereal diseases, as well as rampant recreational drug use, was never fully acknowledged by gay activists, who instead concentrated on those elements that exacerbated the disease, such as the corruption of the medical establishment and the unwillingness of pharmaceutical companies to facilitate potential cures.) This derailing of the gay movement resulted in the disastrous neglect of aesthetics and style, which had always been the great strengths of homosexual culture. AIDS also reduced the gay political agenda in an anti-intellectual, anti-dialectical ontology, also catastrophic considering that ambivalence and paradox had heretofore been one of our most effective strategies. Add to this the fact that, as Fran Lebowitz has pointed out, AIDS killed all the cool people, and it was clear that the gay movement was a sinking ship that us rat finks had to abandon fast.

At this historic moment there was also a stratification of the sexes in the gay scene, and as my closest friends had always been female, I was loathe to betray them. As Don Knotts redux, a weak and flimsy daffodil, and with my unique style, it was virtually impossible for me to get laid in the gay scene anyway, so why stick around? But what was the alternative?

Bored with academia, I started to hang out in the punk scene, which seemed to be characterized by individual style, radical politics, and anarchic behavior—the very tenets of homosexual radicalism that had been lost. Punk not only looked fresh and cool, but politically it was also attempting to rethink how to organize society, decentralize power, and fight corporatization. The early roots of punk were also based on sexual revolution: experimentation with sexual ambivalence, bi- and homosexuality, androgyny, and even gender dysphoria. I started to sport mohawks and accumulate tattoos. I fell in with a group of girls who were already producing music and fanzines and working in Super 8, a cheap and technically simple film format that even a sissy could figure out. We began to show homosexually themed experimental movies in punk clubs and alternative spaces. But imagine our surprise when I started to get jeered at and beaten up by skinheads and mohawks alike for being a fag.

It appears there was a minor complication. By the mid-'80s, punk had stratified into a variety of "-cores," splinter groups with varying agendas. It had always been part of the strategy of punk, in order to evade co-option by the mainstream, to avoid articulating its agenda directly, and to refuse to fix itself on the conventional political spectrum. A flirtation with extreme and disturbing religious or political imagery—Hare Krishna, the bloody cross, the swastika—was designed to be provocative and ambivalent to the point where sometimes personal affiliation to such signifiers became murky. It was the music and style that unified punks, not a reductive, cohesive politic. The advent of hardcore, with its fast, aggressive music and austere, stoic style—shaved head, army boots—ushered in a new machismo, with male bodies flailing in the sweaty mosh pit. Any overt homosexuality was sublimated or repressed. Straight edge, an offshoot of hardcore, even promoted a monkish adherence to self-discipline and self-denial—no drugs, no alcohol, even celibacy. All of this, coupled with the fact that disco fags had become annoying and lame, created a new era of homophobia in punkdom.

So here was poor LaBruce, stuck in exile between two subcultures, unwelcome in both. What was a boy, and several disgruntled girls, to do? Why not start our own little movement? With *J.D.s*, the original queer punk fanzine, we decided to use the punk format—an inexpensive photocopied DIY publication that eschewed copyright and high production values—to push our rebellious homosexual agenda. ("J.D.s" stood for, among other things, Juvenile Delinquents.) And what better way to piss off homophobic punks and skinheads, to ridicule their supposed radicalism, than to get them drunk, take off their clothes, take pictures of their hot, naked bodies, publish them in a fanzine, and distribute it internationally? By embracing pornography, both through stealing from conventional gay porn and by creating our own punk variation, we were paying homage to our queer predecessors, when homosexual was criminal, an underground movement that encompassed all kinds of nonconformist behavior. The shock value also didn't hurt in drawing attention to our little crusade.

As part of our punk training, we had learned from the Situationists the power of the spectacle, of propping up fictions to fight the entrenched ideologies controlling us. Thus we not only created a fanzine but also a movement in full swing, an army of queer boys and girls fed up with the confining roles we were dully expected to fulfill. Another spectacle we created was Bruce LaBruce, my alter ego, a hard-fucking, hard-drinking, out-of-control punk-rock fag who seduces unsuspecting straight and straight-edge boys and leads them into a life of debauchery and vice. I started to appear in the fanzines and our Super 8 home movies, drunk and getting my nipples pierced with a safety pin by my hustler boyfriend, stripping or having my clothes ripped off, or slamming in the pit with my camera, footage that would later be intercut with hardcore gay pornography. But underneath the punk bravado, Don Knotts still secretly lurked.

In the late '8os, a German producer name Jurgen Bruning caught my short movies at an alternative screening, and I approached him to finance a modest, feature-length Super 8 movie. The result was *No Skin Off My Ass*, a loose remake of Robert Altman's *That Cold Day in the Park*, about an effeminate hairdresser who picks up a mute skinhead in the park, takes him home, bathes him, locks him in the guest bedroom, and eventually seduces him. I had already begun to use pornography in the fanzines, so I decided it was time to extend the strategy to celluloid. As I had never had any contact with the porno world proper, it was all trial and mostly error. Despite my somewhat ironic reputation as a porn pinup—an irony, as with Abner Peacock, that people often chose not to read—I was shy and naïve about the mechanics of pornography.

Here's where the Don Knotts syndrome kicked in. Bruce LaBruce was a persona propped up as a sexual spectacle, but it was in some ways a sham, a hoax. As in *The Shakiest Gun in the West* and *The Love God?*, it was also partly engineered by inventive women behind the scenes who developed a strong attachment to the fictional construct. Sitcom complications invariably ensued, not the least of which was myself trying to live up to said spectacle. The movie, originally intended to play in punk venues and alternative art galleries, got picked up on the film festival circuit and started to be screened internationally. Suddenly the sex life of my boyfriend and myself, naïvely committed to celluloid, was being splashed all over the world, which invariably raised doubts about my agenda and questions of profiteering and self-aggrandizement. My response was to throw myself into the persona with gusto. I traveled with the movie for a year, showing up drunk or drugged at engagements, being surly and aggressive in interviews, acting out the ambivalent role of the pierced and tattooed sissy porn star. I quickly realized that once you committed yourself to having sex on film (particularly celluloid, the big screen, the epic scale), especially back in the early '90s, well before the explosion of pornographic imagery in the mainstream, you were regarded differently, as a kind of sexual property. People took liberties with you, touched you inappropriately, treated you as disposable or worthy of contempt even while adoring you, however whimsically.

My next movie, *Super 8½*, shot on 16mm, was a fictionalized cautionary bio-pic about a washed-up porn star named Bruce, an attempt to shoot down the spectacle I had helped to create. The trademark of the porn star I played was his offbeat aesthetic and his unique on-camera style (particularly with his tendency to look directly *into* the camera), which tended to disrupt the illusion of pure pornography, once again drawing attention to the audience's voyeurism. The line between fiction and reality became murky not only for the viewer but for myself, as a Jekyll-and-Hyde persona emerged—or more accurately, a Lewis and Martin: the nebishy sissy versus the Love God, a duality brilliantly articulated in *The Nutty Professor*, in which Jerry Lewis plays both nerdy professor Julius Kelp and smooth heartthrob Buddy Love, a thinly veiled depiction of his former partner, Dean Martin. *Super 8½* ended up becoming another cult item, this time showing at more nongay, international film festivals, culminating in a screening at Sundance. Considering it was a film containing innumerable blowjobs and ass-fucking scenes, this was a quite startling turn of events. The relationship with my boyfriend, which began to crack with *No Skin Off My Ass*, finally ended with his appearance in *Super 8½*, a narrative trajectory that I quickly incorporated into both on- and off-screen spectacles.

For my next movie, I decided I better get the hell out of town. *Hustler White* was shot in 16mm color and documented, in fictionalized form, the swindling male prostitution scene on Santa Monica Boulevard in LA. A loose remake of *Sunset Boulevard* and *What Ever Happened to Baby Jane?*, with a little *Death in Venice* thrown in, it starred former porn pinup and high-fashion model Tony Ward, then well known for his recent high-profile relationship with Madonna. Although *Hustler White* was originally intended to exist in both soft- and hardcore versions, budget and time restrictions prevented us from shooting any hardcore scenes, although we did use several real porn stars in the movie. Through these contacts, and owing to my reputation, I did finally make my

Why knott? A spruce LaBruce, 1994.
Photo courtesy of Bruce LaBruce/Candy Parker

Bruce LaBruce

first forays into the adult video world, visiting porn sets and hanging out with porn icons. *Hustler White* was widely regarded as pornographic owing to its extreme scenes of fetishism—bondage, S&M, mutilation, and, for you amputee lovers, stump-fucking—and because Tony Ward jerks off in the opening scene. The movie, distributed even more widely than my previous two films, was screened at Sundance and Cannes, and in some countries was even blown up to 35mm and sold to television. But at its heart, it was still just another Don Knotts movie, in which my character, a bitchy foreign writer researching hustlers in LA, falls madly in love with the ultimate rent boy. As a critic in *Cahiers Du Cinema* pointed out, in a world imbued with extreme fetishes and sexual violence, the last taboo is tenderness.

At this point in my brilliant career, I was expected in some circles to make the jump to more mainstream filmmaking, but I quickly realized that there may be a glass ceiling for gay pornographers. For this was the reputation I had garnered despite my avant-garde products, which I perceived as being more in line with the experimental movies of such gay directors as Andy Warhol, Jack Smith, and Kenneth Anger. But as that style of avant-garde filmmaking seemed to no longer exist, I decided instead to make my first legitimate porn film. For this momentous occasion, I returned in the late '90s to the theme of my first feature from the early '90s: the gay fetishization of neo-Nazi skinheads. I had come full circle, but the world had changed drastically in the meantime. Pornography had become mainstream, audiences were jaded, and I had more respect for the power of spectacle. A darker, less whimsical pornographic product was in order.

Skin Flick was produced by Berlin's Cazzo Film, a porn production company cofounded by Jurgen Bruning, who had produced all my previous features. (That he himself directs movies for the company under the name Jurgen Anger, the name of my character in *Hustler White*, only reinforces the circularity of it all.) The movie is about a gang of neo-Nazi skinheads that breaks into the home of a bourgeois, mixed-raced gay couple and sexually terrorizes them. As in all my movies, the intersection of race and class with homosexual identity is interpreted in terms of pornographic iconography.

Denounced by some as racist ("Sick Gang-Bang Fantasy" screamed the front page of the *Voice*, a left-wing black London tabloid, while protesters picketed outside the screening at the Institute of Contemporary Art), it was perceived by others as an attempt to redefine and expand the limits of pornography ("An epic of the form," opined *Flash Art International*, calling me "a pornographic Brecht"). The softcore version was screened at innumerable international festivals, straight and gay, while the hardcore version was nominated for nine gay adult video awards in America. In Toronto, the morality squad attended the screening of the softcore version, presented by Pleasure Dome, but deigned not to press charges.

So although I've entered the real world of pornography, albeit through the back door, I still try to see it as an opportunity to exploit a large, undifferentiated mass of representation viewed by millions for my own idealistic, or at least ideological, purposes. Since *Skin Flick* I have shot spreads for a number of porn publications, including *Honcho*, *Mandate*, *Inches*, and *Playguy*, and as of this writing plan on making more porn movies. I'm still the reluctant pornographer, but in this era of rampant assimilationism and gay conservatism, I see pornography as the last refuge of homosexual radicalism. But underneath the glamor of it all, I'm still Don Knotts at heart.

Richard Taylor
Philosopher

You improve your reputation for veracity only slightly by uttering a truth, even a noble one, but be discovered in one deliberate lie, even a small one, and you will never quite be believed again.

Arthur Nersesian
Writer

The Worst Vice

Hundreds of advice books are published every year. Bookstores have advice sections. In these books, "successful" people give their smug secrets to success. These secrets are usually pretty obvious: Get up early, work hard, stay in school, don't take drugs, perse-

No fuck-up: A wise-beyond-his-years Arthur Nersesian.

vere—stuff like that. There's nothing wrong with this advice, but it's not exactly a secret. So many of these books work on prescribed notions of happiness and success. In our society, success is usually reduced to financial gain, sobriety, good looks, popularity, and self-confidence. I have no doubt that money brings many wonderful distractions, but is that true happiness?

Consider those people who live modestly, are insecure, have problem skin, and feel that most of the world is inhabited by dopes. Are they invariably unhappy? Are they failures? I hope not. That pretty much describes most people I know and to a large extent me. I think a lot of people feel unhappy because they don't fit into prescribed notions of happiness. Perhaps the real secret to happiness is not measuring ours against others'. (If only we could do this.)

There are lessons to learn from watching people whom society regards as failures. Recently I saw a homeless guy wearing a T-shirt that read, "The Worst Vice Is Advice." Maybe so. If it teaches little else, the life of failures might demonstrate how elusive good advice can be—and that most people don't want it.

In my search for worthy, pithy, realistic advice, once I got past financial advice that I could have used twenty years ago and is probably worthless now (like "Buy New York real estate"), or odd, quirky advice (I recently heard that Joseph P. Kennedy advised his sons never to pass up an opportunity to get laid), I jotted down some brief, apolitical, nonsexist, multicultural pearls of wisdom. But then I decided to take them out and test them on reality.

"Find something you love to do and stick with it" is good solid counsel. But then I noticed this one man who I've seen for years around midtown. Using the tiny fold-out file on his cheap pair of nail-clippers, he spends his days diligently scraping off notices, political statements, and "for sale" signs taped and glued to aluminum lampposts and corner streetlights.

To him I'd say, aim a tad higher. Try to be a bit more creative. Treat each day like the first day of the rest of your life. That was the catchy jingle for Total cereal. (TV is full of good advice.) And yet I saw this other guy who spends his days finding small fallen trees and carefully chiseling them into a repetition of braids that look like long DNA strands. None of them with any variation or development. He seems happy and maybe that's the point.

I noticed the ligaments in his left hand, particularly his thumb and index finger, with which he holds his chisel. They seemed to have realigned themselves. This too is an interesting lesson.

Even if you don't regard yourself as particularly bright or strong enough to accomplish what you want, stay with it. To some degree, the body and mind adapt to suit their demands. Muscle groups develop and the brain rewires itself in endless ways. I knew a guy who wanted to be a mathematician. He loved the abstract thinking but he was actually bad with numbers. He stuck with it and though he never discovered anything or got hired as a mathematician, he became better at numbers.

Perhaps better advice might be, "Gauge your ambitions with your natural abilities and consider how to utilize whatever opportunities might arise." If you're good at numbers and you work near a beach, try to find something that joins the two, like counting grains of sands. On the other hand, that sounds excruciating. Maybe you should just find something that you like and do that, because life is a long ride and if you have nothing to keep you busy, TV, depression, alcohol, and other nasty habits will fill the void.

Coincidentally, I knew a depressed, TV-watching alcoholic. He lived in my building until he got evicted. He eventually subsisted on collecting refundable cans. He started out just carrying the cans in big shopping bags. I'd see him with his bags of cans lined up at the refund machines outside of the 14th Street supermarket. Gradually, though, ambition kicked in and soon I saw him with a shopping cart, wherein he started collecting other things—items of furniture, prematurely discarded bicycles. His willingness to expand his collection led to larger profits. But when he got more money he drank more, so perhaps, in his case, this advice isn't good either.

But, if can-harvesting is the best you can do, that's okay—it's not like you might have been a brain surgeon or a millionaire (or for that matter are probably even reading this essay).

Twenty-twenty hindsight is always the best advice. In the late 1970s I found myself surrounded by older people who were at the end of their own lives. I had the dubious honor of hearing their regrets. It gave me a perspective very early. Don't live a life that you will end in regret. Inasmuch as each of us have friends and relatives who we respect, and since most problems are so particular and personal, I'd probably suggest asking your own circle of trusted friends for their advice and then choosing the best course.

Advice is important, but no amount of it will keep you from occasionally making a bad move. Bad luck is unavoidable. I knew one fellow who always seemed to make the right choices, but he just had the worst luck. If he was a success at anything, it was his graceful ability to deal with perpetual failure. He used to be chronically late for appointments—perhaps he had a hand in his own bad luck—but he was so good at apologizing it was almost worth it. People very rarely apologize when they are wrong. He didn't blame anyone even when he got screwed out of his modest savings by a telephone con man, and wasted little time on guilt when he missed payments and lost his health insurance. Actually, apologies can be disingenuous

Arthur Nersesian

and perhaps guilt has a function, if only to help you not repeat a mistake.

Perhaps the best advice that I am qualified to give (for those of you who've never heard of me, my best-selling novel is called *The Fuck-Up*) is on how to recover after making a bad move. Forgive yourself quickly, learn something from it, and move on. In my darkest moments, in dealing with great pains, with fear and/or anxiety, I try to move through swiftly, but at the same time step back and remember that life is a sort of roller coaster ride. Sometimes it is wonderful, occasionally it is terrifying. It's all included in the price of the ticket.

Ram Dass
Spiritual leader, writer

Don't sell yourself short by thinking you are only your body or your personality, no matter how intriguing and dramatic they may be. For behind them, there lies a more profound part of your true self. Call it what you will, but . . . call it!

One of the doorways to that higher self is through the cultivation of your intuitive wisdom. As you learn to listen to and trust your intuition, you will find a quiet place in the heart of your being that is wise and can guide your actions. One of the things it will remind you of is your interconnectedness to all things. And out of that appreciation will spontaneously arise compassion for those who suffer, for the earth, and for all living things.

When that happens, don't be overwhelmed by the suffering you see, by the darkness that exists in the human condition. True, there is much of it. But so, too, is there much caring and compassion in the world. Mahatma Gandhi said, "What you do may seem insignificant, but it is very important that you do it." It is important for yourself, as well as for the balances in the world. As you let your compassion guide you into action to help heal the earth and those who suffer, your very acts will feed your own compassionate heart and, in so doing, open the inner gates to knowing your own highest self.

I promise you that plumbing the depths of your being is an unparalleled adventure. I wish you well on the journey.

Jim Harrison
Writer

- Your only true advice is what you've done with your life.

- Speak to your parents occasionally in complete sentences, as it will please them.

- Try to stick to wine over whiskey, as it is easier on the system.

- Don't start smoking, as I've spent an enormous amount of time, energy, and money trying to quit.

- You will lie to others in proportion to how often you lie to yourself, so nip it in the bud.

- The most violent and popular sin nowadays is greed.

- It's not fashionable to think so these days, but you are responsible for what happens to the blacks and Native Americans.

- The natural world is about all we have left of God. What we have done and what we do with the natural world is the measure of our respect for God.

- Cultivate an interest in good literature, art, and music, as it will be a solace for you when everything else fails.

- Don't hit or shoot anybody.

Horst
Photographer

Be guided, but don't copy. Read, listen, and learn from others, then invent. First continue, then begin . . .

Today the world is more open than ever before to all young people, wherever they may be—provided they want to succeed.

The really difficult part is to find out where one's talents lie.

Don't be afraid. One learns through pain, and suffering. Patience helps!

The great German poet, Goethe, said that God gave us the nuts, but that *we* have to crack them.

Self-confidence has nothing to do with self-importance. It has a lot to do with open-mindedness and the capacity to love.

Being clever tempts one to criticize, but doesn't necessarily enable one to create. Creativity has a lot to do with a love of life.

Spend your life searching for beauty in simple—not "fashionable"—things: in an apple, an eye, a body, a bird, or a tree . . .

Keep on wanting to learn.

A Horst is a Horst, of course, of course. The model photographer, age 26.
Photo courtesy Richard J. Horst

William S. Burroughs
Aesthetic terrorist

Words of Advice for Young People

People often ask me if I have any words of advice for young people. Well . . . here are a few simple admonitions for young and old:

Never interfere in a boy and girl fight.

Beware of whores who say they don't want money. *The hell they don't.* What they mean is they want *MORE MONEY,* much more.

If you are doing business with a religious son-of-a-bitch *GET IT IN WRITING.* His word isn't worth shit—not with the good Lord telling him how to fuck you on the deal.

If, after having been exposed to someone's presence, you feel as if you've lost a quart of plasma, avoid that presence. You need it like you need pernicious anemia.

Don't like to hear the word "vampire" around here . . . *trying to improve our public image.*

Build up a *kindly, avuncular, benevolent* image.

INTERDEPENDENCE is the key word.

Enlightened interdependence.

Life in all its rich variety, "take a little, leave a little" . . .

However: by the inexorable logistics of the vampiric process

THEY ALWAYS TAKE MORE THAN THEY NEED.

Avoid fuck-ups.

You all know the type.

Anything they have anything to do with, no matter how good it
sounds, turns into a

DISASTER.

Trouble for themselves and everyone connected with them. A FU is
bad news, and it rubs off—don't let it rub off on you.

Do not offer sympathy to the mentally ill.

Tell them firmly:

I AM NOT PAID TO LISTEN TO THIS DRIVEL.

YOU ARE A TERMINAL FU!

Above all, avoid confirmed criminals. They are a special malignant
strain of FU.

Now, some of you may encounter the devil's bargain if you get that
far. Any old soul is worth saving, at least to a priest, but not *every*
soul is worth buying—so you can take the offer as a compliment.
They try the easy ones first—you know, like money—all the money
there is—but who
wants to be the richest guy in some cemetery?

Money won't buy it.

Not much left to spend it on, *eh Gramps?*

Getting too old to cut the mustard.
Well, "time hits the hardest blows" (*especially* below the belt).
How does a young body grab ya?

Like three card monte. Like pea-under-the-shell.

Now you see it, now you don't.

Haven't you forgotten something, Gramps?
In order to *feel* something you have to *BE there* . . .

You have to *BE* eighteen . . .

You're *NOT* eighteen . . .

You are seventy-eight.
Old fool sold his soul for a strap-on.

Well, they always try the easy ones first.

"How about an honorable bargain"?

"You always wanted to be a doctor, well, now's your chance."

"Why, you could become a great healer and benefit humanity."

What's wrong with that?

JUST ABOUT EVERYTHING.

There are no honorable bargains involving exchange of qualitative merchandise, like souls, for quantitative merchandise like time and money.

So . . . *piss off, Satan,* and don't take me for dumber than I look.

As an old junk pusher told me:

"Watch whose money you pick up."

Devil or angel? William S. Burroughs, age 21.
Photo courtesy of William S. Burroughs
Communications

Wayne Koestenbaum
Writer

Advice to the Young

1. I don't like being in the position of giving advice. So, instead of occupying that unpleasant, bossy role, I will tell you about a humiliating experience that you should avoid replicating in your own life.

2. Come to think of it, I don't want to tell you about that incident.

Born, not made: The rhapsodic, repeat offender Wayne Koestenbaum, age 26, Spring 1985.

3. My hair was sorta cute when I was a college junior, but I didn't know it. My skin was smooth. All I wanted was tough-guy dermis. Now I would like to go back in time and appreciate my own former hair and skin.

4. In 1978 I tried to cruise for sex with guys in the Castro. Nineteen years old, I sat on the steps of a bank and tried to look appealing in my sailor shirt. My attempt to pan for gold came up with naught. Advice: Understand your own cuteness before it is too late and you've lost it.

5. I never approached older powerful people; I thought they'd consider me presumptuous, a young twit. Now I know: Oldsters like to be flattered. So why wasn't I more brave? In the rest room of the Morgan Library I met the great poet James Merrill and he complimented my peacock-blue silk jacket, and what did I say in response? Nothing. I should have followed him to the urinal. Instead I washed my hands and fled. Why didn't I try to pick him up, so I could now be telling my "I slept with James Merrill" story?

6. Premature moral: Utilize your youthful sexiness before it runs dry.

7. I stood beside a record player, listening to Bach or Berg, with a conducting student five years my senior. (I was seventeen.) I'll call him Keith; he might be dead by now. (I looked him up on the Internet. References stopped at 1991.) A mutual friend—a seventeen-year-old girl I'll call Ramona—had said, "Keith is bi." As if bisexuality were news! Ramona had seduced the conducting student. I envied the conquest. I didn't try seducing Keith myself. Perhaps I would have succeeded. At that time I was still a virgin, and didn't have the slightest idea how to lure someone into bed. Keith's slim face appears to me in dreams as an echo of my own, but it was not myself I wished to seduce; I wanted Keith, though he lacked charm. Embracing him would have told me how to endure the next decade, the drunk years, the scholarly and loquacious years, when I wasted half my days talking and the other half hiding. Now I wish I had spent more time listening to contemporary music, and less time making pesto. I suppose I could have listened to contemporary music *while* making pesto. Today I like difficult, recondite works, like Luciano Berio's music for solo piano, which plays on the boombox as I write this essay.

8. I wonder what happened to Keith the conducting student, and why his disappearance matters to me. I only knew him for a few days. We stood near a record player in his dorm room.

9. Keith was also a composer. I never heard any of his pieces. Illegitimate, I existed on the music school's outskirts. Keith, on the other hand, was a star.

10. I admired the fact that Keith had slept with Ramona, my charismatic friend, who had a penchant for gay men. It never occurred to me that Ramona and Keith and I together in bed might have set off sparks.

11. Keith the conducting student: I hardly remember his face. All I see is a sliver of dimness, like hibernation, and a slenderness like my own.

12. Did I say anything seductive to Keith? Did I introduce myself as a sexual being, or did I continue to wear the mask of reticence and dryness?

13. Ramona introduced me to Keith; she wore white turtlenecks, which impressed me because, Californian, I had never seen preppie or ski garb. Keith's slenderness seemed (in advance of any facts) diseased; that summer I was trying to read *Of Human Bondage*, but I never got past the third chapter.

14. Keith acted like an older brother but I didn't want to demolish or overpower him; I didn't want to outshine his accomplishments, or insist he cede his terrorities to my chatty empire.

15. Ramona said Keith's name with a nasal, proprietary tenderness that inspired me to conquer him, though I took no steps toward that victory, and, now, don't know why I call it "conquest" rather than equilateral "friendship." My personality, unfortunately, scars what it passes. And I didn't intend this essay to be a piece of self-reflection. I wanted to give advice to the new generation. I decided to tell youngsters who might not consider themselves physically attractive to give themselves the benefit of the doubt, and to realize that youth was itself an asset. I aimed to encourage novices to move ahead with romantic development, not to hold back.

16. I discovered on the Internet that Keith led a youth orchestra in the late 1980s. His charges must have looked up to slim unaggressive Keith.

17. His real name—lost friend who was never really my friend—has a secret homonymic sympathy with open western spaces, landscapes, like Death Valley, that capture the tourist. His name also is cousin to simultaneity, to the suddenness of thought when it hesitates to announce its departure.

18. I allowed myself to be bossed around when I was young. I listened to my grandfather tell me that classical musicians ended up in the gutter. (Maybe he was right?) I wanted more sensual experience but sat in a cocoon half my own making. Must I convert this essay into a pious valedictory address?

19. I have turned literature, like every love, into a harness. The discursive situations I confront—audience, reader—hold me like a vise, and so I end up not speaking, rather than trying to begin the awful, necessary work of accommodating myself to that confinement, learning the dimensions of prison so I might transform it into a nursery.

20. Schumann's *Album for the Young* begins with a "Melody" that is not exceptionally melodic, and yet it announces itself, brashly, as "Melody." On the Schirmer edition's frontispiece, my first piano teacher wrote: "Rules about the pedal: (1) Not too heavy—use sparingly. (2) Be sure that when you lift pedal, you lift *completely*, then very quickly back down again." I never properly learned how to pedal. Uncertainties over Dr. Spock basics lead me into sloughs of despond, also make sentence momentum difficult. My advice: Continue along your path and refuse to accept diversions, even financial.

21. A haircutter told me in 1979 that I had fine cheekbones, perhaps a falsehood, but I was paying more for that haircut than ever before, and the unisex salon was near a tunnel bisecting the mountain on which our city rested. The tunnel marked the salon's location as a positive place for comprehending my underrated erotic bite. Be precise!

22. All I wanted was hair on my chest. Then hair arrived. Now, boys are shaving their bodies, ridding themselves of natural endowments. Should I shave mine, to return to the state of hairlessness I was eager to flee?

23. Take your intuitions seriously, even if older bossy people tell you that you are deluded and self-indulgent. The word "self-indulgent" (let's destroy it) inhibits breathing.

24. Like Ruth Crawford's "Study in Mixed Accents" (1931) for solo piano, this essay tries to give a pointillist example of how to take seriously one's own ineluctabilities. Much about myself I can't change, even if I tried. And so I try to present the flaws as starkly as possible.

25. I wore an Eiffel Tower earring to a Greenwich Village café and thought myself sexually adventurous, though the earring hurt my earlobe, in winter: frostbite amidst unread Francis Bacon essays and a new consciousness that my genitals could be considered "poison" . . .

26. Giving advice makes me melancholy: Is anyone listening? Will anyone be improved, or moved, by my admissions? Somewhere in my heart there lies, waiting to be described, the time I wanted to sleep with an art-history teacher; we rode together on a bus through an area known as the Fens because of their murkiness, wetness, inaccessibility, beauty, and connection to mythic Irish faerie lore. Darkness out the bus window did not cast aspersions on my failed seduction of the teacher, who ended up prominent in government. His rejection of me was total, though I did not advertise my desire. Almost never have I made a direct erotic proposition; everywhere is feint and fraudulence.

27. Now I am reading about eleventh, ninth, and thirteenth chords in twentieth-century "common practice" composition (clusters, tonal centers, dissonance, restlessness): Knowledge never adds up, and I remain in the dog-paddling mode I occupied twenty-five years ago, a style I should have transcended.

28. If I berate myself in public, will you, reader, reach enlightment and recognize your superiority? Self-laceration—masochism—is a respectable rhetorical strategy.

29. How can I give advice? I am not a father. I am, however, a teacher. My favorite pedagogic trick is to give contradictory promptings that confuse the learner. For example: "Expand the last paragraph, though perhaps its failure to expand is that paragraph's secret strength."

30. Last night I dreamt a cruel former teacher with saggy jowls like an Ingres painting of a dominatrix sat outside a classroom in which my pet students were giving me a "farewell-to-pedagogy" party. One shy and unattractive kid—call him Ken—had nominated himself majordomo of the proceedings. Ken had problems at home: I had indirectly witnessed these difficulties during a parent-teacher conference, when his overweight mother insisted that I describe her son's (nonexistent) accomplishments in great detail. Ken poured me a full cup of tea, which I accepted, because it was part of the "kindness package" he was extending. I had decided to quit teaching, and this, my favorite class, a group of below-average readers and writers, were sorry to see me leave the flock, and wished to toast me. I had been the only teacher ever to diagnose their problems, to sympathize; since I was leaving the profession, they would henceforth lack guide or support in their long journey toward unsatisfactory adulthood, a maturity I am now experiencing, regretting that I cannot correct the flaws or describe them in a fashion that might assist you. In the dream, my cruel teacher, sitting outside the classroom, called me out to join her in the hall of miscreants. There, she pointed toward a telescope and said, "Peer through it." On the lens was a gob of sticky spit or cum; she had not placed the viscous substance on the lens, but she had not objected to its presence, and had not wiped the lens clean for my convenience. Suddenly I had access to a university phone, which it was imperative I use to communicate with my lost father, who might be proud to hear that I, too, was leaving the teaching profession, as he had done several years ago. Again I was thrilled to recognize our similitude, and wished to celebrate it, but was afraid that I had already done so, and that I would be chastised (without probation) for the repetition. Other people in the hallway—large women who resembled Bette Davis or BMW-driving realtors—recognized that my former teacher, the one who had guilt-tripped me into looking through the smudged telescope lens (at what vista? the Golden Gate Bridge?), was a mild lunatic, no longer needing institutionalization, but not to be trusted with forming young minds.

31. Why am I telling you this dream? Because I am a teacher; because I have been instructed to impart wisdom in this essay, and I feel unfit to do so; because, in order to comfort you with stream-lined guidance, I must remember—revisit—images of teachers; because it is painful to do so, bothersome (I hate using the word "pain"). . . .

32. Pat, the dream teacher who mocked me in the hallway, had a husband who knew she was an inadequate legislator, but he was afraid to lead her toward reasonable classroom management practices. I could—in the dream's logic—possibly befriend him, side with him against Pat; the husband and I might exchange bromides, and he might help me reenter the classroom and accept the farewell party, a gift too large and importunate to dismiss. At the party's center was a piece of stale white cake, a year old; unmolested by mice or insects, the cake had kept its shape, but hardened, like a Wayne Thiebaud painting. The classroom cake was not a painting, but I was welcome to confuse it with art; there was no incentive for me to segregate "cake" from "painting of cake"; the two, image and reality, could dwell together, tea-for-two-style, in a cozy cottage by the sea, unbothered by telephone or relation. I began to realize, in the dream, that I could sculpt my fate—grandiose, I considered myself a person with a destiny—and as a consequence of this new self-determination, I began to grow small, as in *Alice's Adventures in Wonderland*, until it seemed I was only a photograph of myself, a miniature pedagogue, with the jauntiness of a child on the way to kindergarten, lunch pail in hand.

33. Each year I had a new, up-to-the-minute lunch pail. TV show spin-offs, the pails had thick thermoses. (Students bought mini cartons of milk for a nickel or dime at lunch hour, and reserved the thermos for juice.) One morning, my thermos contained chocolate milk, but, on that special occasion, I left the lunch pail in a bus headed toward a farm, and so, when I realized the loss, the chocolate milk (growing warm and undrinkable now) seemed the epitome of unattainable treasure, a realm of objects I had forfeited through carelessness.

34. I did not remain vigilant over my possessions, and so, piecemeal, they disappeared. I collected soft-drink bottle caps, and kept them in a shoe box. The collection vanished, or was confiscated—thrown out—by a guardian. Was confiscation wise? I advise you to keep close watch over what you love.

Martha Gellhorn
Novelist, war correspondent

Keep asking *why*. Never stop. *Why, why, why?* Do not believe or obey blindly; be sure you get enough answers to make up your own mind. If you can't get any answers, or only tripe and slogans, then learn to say NO. Your own mind is your best possession; take serious care of it. The State, all States, can make us do a lot of obeying, but not in our minds. Unless you agree fully in your mind and also your heart, you should disagree however you are able. If you follow this simple rule of conduct, you will find that you are often a dissident. Dissidents are a great company of mankind; without them, there would not have been any changes for the better. And since the world is never in perfect shape, it needs as many people as possible asking *why*, thinking for themselves, because that is how some thing are stopped and how some things are started, in every generation.

Perfect shape: Martha Gellhorn, 1943, by Lee Miller.
Photo © Lee Miller Archives

Lucius Shepard
Writer

When I was fifteen I was arrested for stealing a car. Since I was no hardened criminal, the authorities decided to teach me a lesson by sticking me in the county jail overnight before sending me home. They put me in a two-person cell with this guy about ten or twelve years older than me. His name was Randy something. He had long hair, tattoos, and a meanly handsome face, and he was headed for the state prison at Raiford, where he had been sentenced to do a five-spot for burglary.

"But I won't serve more'n two," he said. "Two's a fuckin snap."

Though in retrospect I can see that Randy was just another jail-house punk, though I understand now that he talked to me not to pass on any wisdom but to shore himself up, to stop himself from thinking about the bad dogs waiting for him up in Raiford, at the time he seemed a romantic figure, dangerous and canny, and I took what he said to heart. He told me how it was to be a thief, how to get past locks and alarms, how to select a target house, what sort of tools were required for state-of-the-art B&E.

"You can do a helluva lot worse than second-story work," he said. "Sure, you probably gonna get popped once or twice, but that's how it goes with fuckin' everything, right? Even stockbrokers have to take a fall sometimes. Even presidents and shit. But the thing is, man, it's a very cool feeling to have more'n chump change in your pockets, y'know, with some fine merchandise in the back of your car for when times are thin. You're livin' it, man! And the ladies, they feel it in ya; they like to be around that kind of action. But just 'cause you doin' crime, man, just 'cause you walkin' on the edge, it don't mean you ain't gotta do the right thing. When you see them cherrytops comin', run like hell but don't hurt nobody. You get ahead of the game, let some of your money loose out in the world where it can do some good, 'cause chances are that good thing'll come back around sometime. And when you go for a score, know your crime partner, man. Make

sure you know that sucker to the bone! He's all that's standin'
between you and some bad life experiences. And if you get away with
it, don't hang onto shit that can bring you down later. Take the cash
and flush the credit cards. Ain't no piece of plastic with another man's
name on it ever gonna get you a big win."

I've never been much good at taking advice. I guess I believe
that people are better off following their instincts and ignoring the
bullshit that clamors for their attention, the sales pitches and the
quasi-Christian pleas of TV hustlers and the "buy me" speeches
made by three-piece politicians who do it to the public doggie style
and never lose that winning smile. I find it hard to accept that you
would want to hear me or anyone else prattle on about What Must Be
Done. Nor can I accept that there is a great will in the United States
toward effecting the changes that will permit our survival. Revolution is something made by desperate men and women, and usually
desperation comes too late. We in this country are insulted by pros-
perity against the symptoms of the afflictions that should long ago
have bred desperation in us. Time is not on our side, and thus the
offering of advice, no matter how enlightened, seems futile. However, on the off-chance that my cynicism has blinded me to some
subtle new reality, I might as well chip in my two cents' worth.

If we are to remove earth from the Endangered Planets list, I
think it likely that a substantial number of you will have to live lives
of restraint and sacrifice, that you will have to forego to a large
extent the greedy rush for power and position and various other
gratifications that generally typify one's postgraduate years in
America. You may be called upon to choose between personal security and the satisfaction of making an effort, of putting back into the
society something of the vitality that has been drained from it by
your predecessors. It is quite possible that you will have no choices,
that the quality of life in the United States will slide rapidly and
drastically downhill, and that you will be forced into activism in
hopes of reversing the process. But if choices remain to you, then
you will require sound information upon which to base your judg-

ments, and you cannot rely upon the government or the media to provide it. The majority of newspapers and television news programs have no more correspondence with the real world than does *Lara Croft: Tomb Raider.* They have become propaganda organs whose function is to manipulate, to soothe, to compose via the scripted dialogue of some blow-dried creep the government-sponsored view of a humanity beset by a handful of serious problems (problems that the Bad Breath Committee on Armchair Disarmament and other august bodies are, we're led to believe, working night and day to resolve), rather than showing the medium of chaos and despair in which we actually exist.

For instance, the media has told us nothing lately concerning El Salvador, a country where one fifth of the population has become refugees and where, under the stewardship of Duarte and Christiani, the atrocities committed by the death squads reached unparalleled extremes; nor have we heard much about the genocidal acts committed by Idi Amin's successors in Uganda (perhaps his successors did not have the sensationalist appeal of that cannibal president); nor have we heard a great deal about the human rights violations taking place on a prodigious scale in Guatemala, Chile, Argentina, and a dozen other bastions of terror, and what we *have* heard has been force-fed to the media by groups such as Amnesty International and is usually buried as filler on page thirty-two of your local paper's Living section. So, to understand fully the ways of the world you will either have to revolutionize the media, become journalists and enforce the publication of real news and substantive commentary—a challenging task, as many journalists will tell you—or else you will have to abandon it utterly and seek new methods of disseminating information.

It may not seem personally relevant to keep track of what is happening in these faraway lands, but if you do you will begin to have a sense of how thoroughly you are being lied to and how near the edge of disaster the average human being is living. And you also will see clearly how this process of disinformation permits withered, hormoneless thumb-puppets like George W. Bush and Dick Cheney to ascend to power. The cornerstone of a successful democracy is an informed populace, and because we have let ourselves grow uninformed, we have licensed a dynasty of third-raters to govern our lives. We can no longer issue such a license if we hope to survive. We can no longer allow ourselves to be fuddled by political sleights-of-hand. We must recognize that an action like the invasion of Panama had not the slightest effect in reducing drug abuse and was merely a diversion to keep our minds off the matter at hand and to score points in the popularity polls among those foolish enough to believe that America needs Sly Stallone in the White House. To point up what I am saying, I urge you to take note of the various public debates regarding the virtues of our current adventure in the Middle East. Too often they resemble unenlightened brawls, such as I recently witnessed on CNN's *TalkBack Live*, where Arab-Americans contended with rabid patriots thirsting for Afghan blood. Not a one of these people had more than the most simplistic of worldviews. They spoke in slogans, in headlines, and their speech was funded not by reason but by the most wrongheaded and doctrinaire of emotions: righteous outrage. That sort of dialogue serves only the fools who have led us to this pass. To overcome the decades of indulgence and self-absorption that have neutered our collective intelligence and reduced our national will to a brutish exercise in cheerleading, you must succeed in gaining sufficient information to recognize the betrayals of the public trust that our government and governments all over the world have perpetrated and continue to perpetrate. Then and only then will you be able to make an informed decision as to whether you wish to surrender to what seems inevitable, to seize all the happiness and security you can, or if you want to attempt to be happy by working for a common good, which is generally held to be the more fulfilling of the two courses, yet is by far the road less traveled.

It is to you who make this latter choice that I wish to offer advice. Not my advice, but that of the thief whom I met in the Volusia County Jail when I was fifteen. I believe that you who seek to res-urrect the world will be mightily hard-pressed in the years ahead, that you will need to be strong and defiant and perhaps will risk being outlawed, that you may in effect have to steal love and joy from the menacing circumstance of the twenty-first century, and the thief's words strike me as embodying a code that you may have to obey in order to earn a victory of the spirit over the oppressions of injustice, inanition, and the moral cowardice of nations. I wish I could offer you something inspirational, something about love and beauty, but although I set great store by those qualities, I do not think they are terribly pertinent at this time.

So, my advice to you is as follows . . .

Just because you're living on the edge doesn't mean that you don't have to do the right thing.

Run like hell if you have to, but try not to hurt anyone.

If you get ahead of the game, let some of your money loose in the world where it can do some good, and chances are that good thing will come back around.

Make sure you know whomever you have to trust.

Take the cash and flush the credit cards.

Lucius Shepard

Alain de Botton
Writer, philosopher

Having only recently reached thirty, it seems more than usually presumptuous to give anyone advice on life. However, I can perhaps allow myself a few words about the twenties—in light of how ill-prepared most late-teenagers seem to be about how awful this decade can be.

De Botton can change your life.

If these are anxious years, it's perhaps because they present hitherto undreamt-of possibilities for ruining one's life. In previous decades, one might have chosen a boring subject in college or kissed someone unsuitable. But by the age of thirty, if things have gone somewhat wrong, you could, for instance, realize you'd married the wrong person *and* chosen the wrong career. Hence, the anxiety, the sign of heated efforts to avoid danger.

Of course, it wasn't supposed to be like this. The problems were supposed to end along with adolescence—that was the time reserved for resolving parental conflicts, determining the meaning of life, and acquiring an adult identity free of confusion and complexes. But the struggles commonly attributed to adolescence are, it seems, more often played out in the twenties. These are the years in which a practical meaning to life has to be forged, when idealism comes into contact with oppressive realities (the gas bill), when the point of relationships has to shift from kissing to starting a family, and when identity becomes linked to job and salary.

It starts with the end of education. Up until then, one can rest cozily in the status of a student. The world doesn't expect much of students. They can be badly dressed, poor, illogical, pretentious, and moody. How quaint these traits are. Students are, after all, merely a welter of possibilities, butterflies in chrysalises, and adults are liable to look generously upon their foibles—foibles that no longer look so cute at twenty-five, and are plain appalling at thirty. Perhaps the greatest shock of the twenties is that one's estimation in the eyes of others becomes linked to worldly achievements. It is no longer enough just to have a winning smile and a warm personality; one is now judged according to rank in a new and terrifying pecking order. Perhaps for the first time, one can be made to feel a "nobody"—because this is also the age when, for the first time, one is offered opportunities to be a "somebody." One might naturally reject worldly values (a venerable tradition ever since Socrates walked barefoot around Athens and urged his fellow citizens to care for their souls, not their possessions), but one can't ignore that worldly values are the ones most people will be using to weigh up one's worth.

To resist worldly pressures requires courage and self-belief. It is easy to play the rebel at fifteen (it is even expected), far more difficult at thirty; it is difficult to abandon the expectations of the world and the safety of a conventional career path in order to try and become, for instance, a violinist, stand-up comedian, or entrepreneur—projects that attract painful scorn and sarcasm unless they can be realized.

At the same time, a peculiar thing starts to cast its shadow on every aspect of the personal life: marriage. The question "Where is this going?" presses in on couples and dissolves a sizeable number of them, the options being either toward a wedding ceremony and children, or eventual breakup. Gone is the earlier, almost automatic assumption that a romantic involvement could not sensibly culminate in marriage. Now, for many, there is little point accepting a dinner date, learning baby talk, and agreeing to a weekend in Paris unless there is at least a serious chance this will end at the registry office.

It's easy to grow depressed at the sheer unlikelihood of finding a suitable mate, particularly late at night, on returning from yet another barren social engagement. The chances of bumping into a desired creature are about as remote as bumping into an acceptable flat without the help of a real-estate agent (and then, securing the flat presents a host of the most draining challenges). Until computer dating agencies become a more accepted feature of social life (my prediction for the twenty-first century) or the arranged marriage makes a comeback (charming but unlikely), it seems we will have to continue the absurd system of relying on luck to land a partner with whom to spend the rest of existence. People will continue going to parties in the vain hope that somewhere between the kitchen and the stereo, Mr. or Ms. Good Enough will be standing, eagerly waiting to have their romantic lives transformed. (The high divorce rate must at least in part be explained by the number of people who despaired of ever finding the right person, and hence plumped for someone halfway unsuitable.)

The shadow of marriage changes the romantic pecking order. Qualities that facilitate a good marriage and the rearing of children start to weigh more heavily. In this writer's modest experience, life becomes somewhat easier for gauche, peculiar-looking men in their twenties. It no longer matters so much if they are unattractive, as long as they aren't grossly insensitive and unpleasant. The reckless-but-exciting rock guitarist gradually becomes a less enticing proposition for the long-term, and one can see on the arms of many women of twenty-eight the sort of physically challenged male to whom she would not have given the time at fifteen, but now loves tirelessly. And in case all this seems absurdly trivial, take it from Schopenhauer, who knew that nothing could be more important: "Love is quite worthy of the profound seriousness with which everyone pursues it. What is decided by it is nothing less than the composition of the next generation."

Most of the miseries that occur in later decades, most of those blandly labeled "midlife crises," can be traced to wrong decisions taken in one's twenties. If one is leading a conscious and examined life, it is perhaps inevitable, and even desirable, that this should be a worrying time.

Dan Jenkins
Writer

Don't be too upset because a twelve-year-old has won the National Book Award for fiction with a novel titled *Love Songs of an Albino Dwarf.* After all, it only sold three copies in New York and one in Seattle.

Don't be too upset because a sixteen-year-old albino dwarf is named president and CEO of AOL–Time Warner–Newsweek–Vanity Fair–Fox–Germany–Japan–Turner–Pepsi–Dell–Nissan–Viacom–Sports Illustrated–Krispy Kreme.com.

Choose your friends carefully. Many of the people you know in high school and college will wind up selling insurance.

Friends are more important than family. Close friends won't criticize your behavior, and as you grow older you will realize that your close friends are really your family. You chose them—you didn't get to choose your family, many of whom are deadbeats.

Work at something you enjoy and work for the sheer pleasure of it; money will be a fringe benefit.

Say no to network television. Live on cable. Say no to music videos.

Assassinate rap every chance you get.

A sense of humor will dig you out of a lot of life's ditches. If you don't have a sense of humor, order one off the computer. Remember: Laughter is the only thing that will cut trouble down to a size where you can talk to it.

Support freedom of choice in all things.

Martha Nussbaum
Philosopher

Do not despise your inner world. That is the first and most general piece of advice I would offer to a generation of Americans. Our society is very outward-looking, very taken up with the latest new object, the latest piece of gossip, the latest opportunity for self-assertion and status. But we all begin our lives as helpless babies, dependent on others for comfort, food, and survival itself. And even

Martha, Martha, Martha: Nussbaum as a college freshman.

though we develop a degree of mastery and independence, we always remain alarmingly weak and incomplete, dependent on others and on an uncertain world for whatever we are able to achieve. As we grow, we all develop a wide range of emotions responding to this predicament: fear that bad things will happen and that we will be powerless to ward them off; love for those who help and support us; grief when a loved one is lost; hope for good things in the future; anger when someone else damages something we care about. Our emotional life maps our incompleteness: A creature without any needs would never have reasons for fear, or grief, or hope, or anger. But for that very reason we are often ashamed of our emotions, and of the relations of need and dependency bound up with them. Perhaps males, in our society, are especially likely to be ashamed of being incomplete and dependent, because a dominant image of masculinity tells them that they should be self-sufficient and dominant. So people flee from their inner world of feeling, and from articulate mastery of their own emotional experiences. The current psychological literature on the life of boys in America indicates that a large proportion of boys are quite unable to talk about how they feel and how others feel—because they have learned to be ashamed of feelings and needs, and to push them underground. But that means that they don't know how to deal with their own emotions, or to communicate them to others. When they are frightened, they don't know how to say it, or even to become fully aware of it. Often they turn their own fear into aggression. Often, too, this lack of a rich inner life catapults them into depression in later life. We are all going to encounter illness, loss, and aging, and we're not well prepared for these inevitable events by a culture that directs us to think of externals only, and to measure ourselves in terms of our possession of externals.

What is the remedy for these ills? A kind of self-love that does not shrink from the needy and incomplete parts of the self, but accepts those with interest and curiosity, and tries to develop a language with which to talk about needs and feelings. Storytelling plays a big role in this process of development. As we tell stories about the lives of others, we learn how to imagine what another creature might feel in response to various events. At the same time, we identify with the other creature and learn something about ourselves. As we grow older, we encounter more and more complex stories—in literature, film, visual art, music—that give us a richer and more subtle grasp of human emotions and of our own inner world. So my second piece of advice, closely related to the first, is: Read a lot of stories, listen to a lot of music, and think about what the stories you encounter mean for your own life and the lives of those you love. In that way, you will not be alone with an empty self; you will have a newly rich life with yourself, and enhanced possibilities of real communication with others.

YES, BURN YOUR BRIDGES!

BY BETTE DAVIS

READING TIME
9 MINUTES 25 SECONDS

Bette Davis, Hollywood's poised and glamorous star, was once a self-conscious girl, afraid of smiling.

Here's daring advice to youth from

EVER since you were a child you've heard the warning of your elders: "Don't burn your bridges behind you. You never know when you may want to go back."

But after having had to live the most vital ten years of my life on quite a different basis, I say, *Burn your bridges!* That is, if you really want to be a success. It's the best way I know of *not* going back.

Don't leave yourself any avenue of retreat. No comforting alibis or faithful stand-bys, such as the old job back again, just "in case" you don't like the new path or are not making a go of it. Instead of securing your position, as you think, you'll be weakening it inestimably.

I can remember when I burned my first big bridge. I was just finishing a run in Solid South with Richard Bennett. For two years picture offers had been cropping up, but I had steadfastly refused the idea of Hollywood.

Why? Fear, of course. I knew all too well how many budding young Broadway things had tripped out to the movie capital with visions of embedding themselves in the firmament of stars, only to land on a nice reserved upper shelf of some company's darkroom. What was to prevent my landing there?

There was the additional consideration of finances. How long, given a bad run of luck, could I sustain myself, my mother, and my sister? Had I the right to risk their welfare?

Or was I using all of these as alibis to cover a deeper reason? Was the underlying explanation for my Hollywood qualms the fact that I was horribly camera-shy? All my life I'd had a phobia about standing in front of a camera, probably because of my saucer eyes, and long neck, and teeth that had been a constant struggle to straighten. Think what a professional life of living in front of a lens would mean to such a person.

I finally decided the last was the honest answer, and the others were just fine-sounding dodges; that, if for no other reason than licking the coward inside of me, I'd better accept Universal's offer.

When the time came for my test, I walked in front of the camera and fell in a dead faint on the floor! Sheer fright. The absurdity of the whole thing—that any one who could shout her lungs out before a thousand people

without turning a hair should pass out cold at the sight of a little ground glass in a black box—generated a fury in me that was better than any spirits of ammonia. Raging mad, I picked myself up, asked the pardon of the astounded crew, and proceeded with the test. From that day to this I haven't repeated the performance. The fright seemed to get out of my system in that one cataclysmal moment. So there was one bridge well burned.

But no, say our elders, don't be too hasty. You may want to go back.

Well, who wants to go back? I'll tell you. The failures. The people, for instance, who are terrified when a chance comes to go on into a new and exciting kind of work that they have never done before. They make a great show of going on, but all the while they're doing a lot of roadwork on the path that leads to the past—old friends, old associations, old work. They devote so much creative energy to preparing a soft bed to land on in the event they're kicked out of the new job that they haven't enough energy left to make a success of it. So they hurriedly fail in the new field and turn with a sigh of relief to the road back.

8

Poor things. If only they knew, if only we could all realize, there isn't any road back. We may fondly believe it leads back through the old familiar places, but we don't stop to reckon that it can, at best, be but a parallel course, like a mountain trail that doubles back on itself in hair-pin turns, and the road itself may be rough and danger-ous, leading to the swamps below.

I remember when I was headed for the swamps below after my first unhappy year in Hollywood. The option on my contract was up and Universal was letting it drop.

Not that I blame Universal. If I had been Carl Laemmle I should have done just what he did—can me. In fact had I been confronted with what faced him when I walked on the set for my first picture I would have stopped the cameras and sent for the accident insurance. Think of it. In a town where beauty is the Ten Com-mandments I dared to appear without a scrap of make-up on my face or an inch of curl in my hair! I did more than dare; I flatly refused to appear any other way. The part I was to take was that of a wallflower, and I main-tained it should be clearly evident why I was a wallflower. It was!

I remained a sort of studio wallflower; wouldn't make friends, wouldn't even smile—again on account of my teeth—until one bright and shiny day Ray Jones told me a funny story and snapped a picture of the result.

"There!" he announced, slapping the photograph down in front of me two days later. "Do you see why I want you to smile?"

The hour had struck for me at Universal. I was on the road back, but I wasn't deluding myself with the idea that it was the same one on which I came out. This time there was a perceptible drop in the trail. Suddenly I realized I had actually fought to fail! Wouldn't do this, wouldn't do that, wouldn't do the other. And what a lot of energy these wouldn'ts had taken! I could have suc-ceeded with half of what it took to fail!

Then, why not succeed instead of fail?

Once before, when I was sixteen, I had learned the bit-ter lesson that failure is a costly device. It was after Eva Le Gallienne turned me down for her Manhattan Civic Repertory School because I wasn't sincere enough in my attitude toward the theater. You couldn't appreci-ate what that pronunciamento meant to me without know-ing that on the strength of my faith in my career, my mother had cut away family ties (speaking of burning bridges!) to be with me and lend her support. It meant the end of help to us from my father's side. His family was unalterably opposed to any such wildcat scheme. There was no going back for her. But I wasn't any good.

r who knows — because she's tried it

America's top-ranking actress had said so. Every door in life, I felt, was closed to me. How was I to make it up to mother for her sacrifice?

What happened was that mother, as usual, made it up to me. Undaunted by the unpromising situation, she struck up into Connecticut and took over a photograph studio. Due to her industry, the little studio kept our bodies and souls glued together while I lay in a complete funk for six months, trying to get my scattered bearings; the six blackest, blankest months of my life.

There and then I learned life doesn't like failures. You're out of line, and it keeps pushing and kicking you, trying to force you back into the groove that lands all the balls in the winning pocket.

Again it was mother who found the groove. At the end of six months she took a long look at her daughter and said, "I think we'll go to John Murray Anderson's Dramatic School in New York." She earned my tuition by taking a job in a girls' school.

But how, reverting to my Universal dilemma, was I to turn failure into success at this late date? Everything was over but the whistle of the train going back East.

It was then that I asked for my chance to do a good job. Asked and asked! ". . . and ye shall receive." When the miracle of George Arliss' requesting me for The Man Who Played God came to pass on the eve of my departure from Hollywood, I knew I had "received."

Take my word, it's a lot easier to succeed than to fail—and I've done both. You have to fight all the time to maintain failure. You have to withstand a hundred de-pressing thoughts a day. You have to contend with the humiliation, not to mention the actual physical depriva-tion, of being broke. No, thanks; not for mine.

Success, on the other hand, carries you along on its own momentum. Once the hard part of getting it started is over, it generates its own power as it goes. It's stimu-lating, exciting.

I don't mean to say that all you have to do for success is open the window and let it fly in. It doesn't come un-asked, unearned, unimpeded. You sweat; in any walk of life you sweat for it. You rack your wits for it and take some terrible chances for it. You slash out the back roads and hang yourself out on the end of any number of limbs for it.

(And still I say it's easier than failure!)

I REMEMBER one limb of mine that reached all the way across the Atlantic and dangled me in England. When I walked up the gangplank of the Empress of India, I knew there was no turning back. Yet there was a great and abiding virtue in the very finality of the situation. It ended the agonizing indecision, and I have observed that indecision is a most dangerous mental luxury. Mull-ing over the pros and cons, and trying to figure out what would happen if you followed this course or that course, produces a sort of brain jam—which requires something in the nature of T. N. T. to dynamite it into action again.

So I've worked out a routine for handling decisions on important matters: Think it out as clearly as you can, do it, and drop it.

The most important of these is to drop it. No one can be one hundred per cent right in all the decisions to be made throughout a lifetime. We're bound to make mistakes. But, by the simple process of dropping it, we can prevent a bad decision ruining the rest of our lives.

Before we leave entirely that limb that dangled me in England, I'd like to correct a statement attributed to me. That statement said that money was the root of the diffi-culty. On the contrary, I never at any time had an argument with my studio on anything but parts. You can rely on the source of this information.

But now you'll ask if I can honestly say the theory of burning one's bridges has worked in my own case. The answer is that I can. And, hazardous as is the practice of prescribing one's own remedies for another person's perplexities, I still have faith enough to want to pass the idea along for the help it can give.

Try it. Not on your biggest and most vital problem first. Try it on one of the lesser ones.

For instance, if you're a woman, maybe you've been in a funk over which dress to wear to an important party. Perhaps you've been thinking about it at odd moments for days, wasting unmeasured amounts of time and energy on it. Well, just line up the possible candidates and give yourself a maximum of ten minutes by the clock in which to decide. Believe me, dress or no dress, nothing is so important to you as breaking that habit of mental waste. After you've made your decision you'll find your mind will shoot on to other problems and tackle them with added vigor.

Or maybe you're a man, and the question isn't one of clothes, but of a job you'd give your eyeteeth for, if—Just hitch all those ifs together. Then touch a match to one end of the chain. As the fire leaps across the chasm below and you realize your uncertainties have gone up in smoke behind you, you'll feel a surge of new power. Then there's only one way open—AHEAD.

Don't burn your bridges behind you? A grandmother's tale for those who like to have their failures suitably sponsored.

I burned mine. Why not you?

And may you make a roaring success of it!

THE END

Bette Davis

Rita Dove
Poet

Advice to the Young Writer

I remember many a restless night when, unable to sleep, I reached for a book to keep the hounds of anxiety away. Miraculously, a poem or a character in a novel would reach out and soothe me. In a way, those poems and those characters gave me the best advice possible: They counseled me in my need by telling me their stories; they offered me the example of their lives. Advice by example is the only kind I seem to take to, and it's the only kind I can give. Though what follows talks about the condition of being a poet, I think anything we love and want to excel in bears with it the same doubts and challenges. Why does anyone ever aspire to be a poet? On the one hand, writing poetry is one way of singing, of molding the ache of life into a beautiful shape. On the other hand, writing *is* a way of connecting, of calling out "Who's there?" in hope of an answer. A semaphore, a flare, a message in the bottle—a thread of thought to others which reassures us that even in the least illuminated corners of our psyches *we are not alone*.

Even if you've decided that, yes, poetry is what you want to do, for a long time the unasked question is: "Am I on the right track; is my writing good?" The answer is: Who knows? You see, no one can tell you that, and it doesn't matter, since you won't believe them anyway. It seems to me that if you get joy and satisfaction out of the process of writing—if writing and rewriting sustains you even when you're cursing the writing—then no number of setbacks or prizes can substitute for that pleasure. No matter how many books you may publish, how many detractors you might attract, there is always the next blank sheet of paper, the next unsayable urge. And I'm not saying that writing poetry is always a pleasure, that it isn't heart-wrenching and backbreaking. If life doesn't get easier, why should writing?

So, what's one to do? If you find yourself despairing, talk to others about it. Read to remind yourself that you are not alone.

And stay curious. . . .

Steve Stern
Writer

Offhand I would say, along with Pynchon's Benny Profane, that I haven't learned a goddamn thing. But somewhere along the way I did stumble across this dubious bit of information. I discovered quite accidentally that, when our grandparents came to this country, they brought a lot of baggage. They brought with them, along with various superstitions, an assortment of devils and angels, the odd denizens of eternity that had inhabited their native lands. In the end, like everyone else, these creatures became assimilated. They dropped their standards and took up with each other, with mortals, until men and women and devils and angels were all indistinguishable in our streets, a single race. After a couple of generations we even managed to forget, conveniently, that we were the spawn of such awful and wonderful unions, the products of illicit mixed marriages between the celestial and the terrestrial, not to say the infernal—the miscegenation of eternity and time.

Crikey! Steve Stern going bolshie in Brighton, 1970.

Maybe I do us all a disservice to recall the shame of our impure origins. But on the other hand, I can say that it's been some solace to me, as I hope it may be to you, to remember that we are at least more than meets the eye.

Fay Weldon
Writer

Well, there are the ordinary acceptable strictures to offer—such as do your exams and raise yourself above the herd (poor herd, what about them!); don't marry young; don't have children before you're twenty-five; recognize that love is a fine and exhilarating emotion but not one to trust your future to; understand that employment is an unnatural and immoral matter (your employer offers you work on grounds that he can make a profit out of you—where's the dignity in that?) and unemployment is a depressing business and few people can enjoy idleness for long—but I think there is something more interesting to be said to the young. It's this:

Develop your aesthetic sensibilities: not just in the material world, but in the activities that go on in your own head—so you can say of your own emotions, your own actions, this is graceful, that is not; this attractive, that ugly; I will pursue the former, eschew the latter. That something feels right is a sounder guide than what is conventionally held to be proper behavior. So often the choices are not between good and bad anyway, but between the lesser of evils, in which there are no precedents to guide us, only this aesthetic sensibility which I write of. I perceive, I feel, I somehow know that this action, this statement is better than that, just as I know that this is a well-designed sofa, better than that one, because I've practiced *looking*.

As to how these sensibilities are developed—well, that's different, I grant you. You may well be surrounded by ugly wallpaper, crude patterns, concrete alleys, dirt, dereliction, decay—a world that, in despair, seems to value ugliness over grace. But there are paintings in galleries, poems in books; there is music on the radio. Houseplants, studied, can offer food for thought, a suggestion of the natural underlying grace of all things. Once the best is known and understood, what is second best or worse is more easily recognized. Mind you, concentration is required: a turning off of television sets.

A walk in the country, half an hour contemplating the heavens on a starry night, can do more to fit you for civilized and animated company than, say, an A grade in geography, and you live the more easily with yourself, and the more interestingly with others. Understand that Mickey Mouse is cute but appalling and Goofy is an assault on human dignity, and you've begun.

Murray Bookchin
Radical

I have been a radical throughout my entire life as a thinking person, and I shall probably remain one up to the very end. Having reached the age of eighty, I would like to suggest what others may be able to learn from my experiences.

At a time when people have become more pragmatic in their thinking and are concerned primarily with their careers— often at the expense of any ideals or vision

The young Turk, Murray Bookchin.

of life as a creative adventure—I find that the most sustaining factor in my own life has been that very idealism that so many people tend to avoid. I have seen people from my own generation, going back to the 1920s and 1930s, surrender their principles and their commitment to social change; few of them, if any, have since found their lives meaningful. Ironically, the fullest life in a deeply personal sense may well be one that is guided by ideals, by the visions that many people today regard as utopian, and by ethics, which is currently so often discarded in favor of practical realism.

What has sustained me in these eighty years and given my own life meaning is association with other human beings in a common struggle for social freedom; a belief in the marvel of human potentialities; and adherence to a radical ethics based on creativity and the need to create a rational society. Without my lifelong commitment to study, my passionate devotion to ideas, my unceasing curiosity in the marvel that constitutes humanity, I might have very well had a materially good life, but it would have been a vacuous one.

For me, the continual study of ideas, the continual pursuit of knowledge, and an everyday effort to change society in such a way that we live in harmony with each other and with the natural world, has given me the richest kind of personal life as well as the most socially meaningful way of life. In 1968, in May-June, when the students of Paris rose up to try to change the mediocre world in which they lived, they raised the cry, "I love revolution because it is the best way to live." After these many decades that cover the greater part of the twentieth century—including the 1930s (the Great Depression, the era of labor upsurges), the Second World War, and the 1960s—I can honestly say that the Parisian students' slogan is true for me in the deepest personal as well as social sense.

We are only visitors on this planet, transient beings who are here perhaps for only a moment—and the highest way of life, the deepest commitment to social ideas, the most radical visions of a free future, are too often bartered away for a life of mediocrity filled with petty egoism, small-minded materialism, and cold indifference to the human and natural condition. We must not allow ourselves to be juvenilized and trivialized.

I have also learned that it is important not only to adhere to one's ideals but to fully and consistently think out one's ideas. In a time when television gives us one-dimensional images of human experience and mere shadows of the vibrant reality around us, it is easy to leave one's ideas incomplete and be satisfied with half-finished thoughts. I repeatedly encounter people who start from a basic point but never fully think out its consequences. But an unfinished thought is dangerous; it may lead us in any direction, even in directions contrary to our original intentions. For example, I have been involved in ecology issues since 1952, when the word "ecology" was practically unknown even to educated people. Unless one thinks out what ecological politics means—to the consequent fact that all our ecological problems stem from social problems— our commitment to ecology can be used for totalitarian purposes as easily as for liberatory ones. I recall well that romantic views of nature involving a love of one's soil, one's "Volk," and even animals produced a Nazi ideology based on nationalism, racism, and imperialism. Such an ideology was possible in part because people did not think out fully the problem of humanity's place in the natural world.

Our ideas must always be completed, fully thought out, and richly informed by a knowledge of the past. To separate oneself from the past, to maintain a sense of mere nowness, to deny what reason has to give us, as well as intuition, and most dangerously to leave one's thoughts unfinished, is to risk the grave dangers of manipulation and ignorance.

Today we are faced with a counter-Enlightenment that eschews thought, rationality, and even history and individuality. It is disempowering us, as surely as are the vast bureaucracies, corporations, and states that pervade our everyday lives. We must regain a new idealism and a new ethical commitment, and seek self-empowerment through communities and movements for social change. Being destroyed by this counter-Enlightenment are the great human possibilities that make us into truly individuated, dedicated, rational, and socially committed human beings.

The new Enlightenment that we seek involves not only the recovery of a truly organic or dialectical form of reason, a new liberatory politics, new ecologically oriented communities and technologies, and an ethics of social commitment, but also, at the same time, the recovery of our very personhood, individuality, and powers as free individuals who take control over their own destiny.

This body of beliefs has not only guided me through decades of war and social upheaval; it has given me a life more meaningful, purposive, and creative than any of the materialistic careers, narcissistic egotism, or therapeutic techniques so fashionable today could have done.

John Zerzan
Activist

Whose Future?

My advice or exhortation is the same to everyone, but especially to you who have the most to lose: Fight back.

We're on a death march, with the destination coming into clear view. Bill Joy, founding CEO and chief scientist of Sun Microsys-

He's da bomb: Uni-versally friendly anti-civilization theorist Zerzan, mid-seventies.

tems, says we have maybe thirty years before genetic engineering, nanotechnology, and robotics become fully self-replicating. The high-tech Brave New World will then rule us directly.

One hundred species of plant and animal life go extinct every day, and that number continues to inch upward. The oceans are dying. Proliferating studies tell us that global warming, increasing steadily, will kill the biosphere within a few decades. Ozone holes get bigger, and cancer has become epidemic as air, water, and soil become increasingly toxic.

From the age of two, children are now liable to be prescribed Ritalin and/or antidepressants to drug them into compliance with an ever more empty, unhealthy life-world. Kids shooting kids at school has become almost as commonplace, joining the horror of multiple-homicide rampages at home, work, or Burger King. The teenage suicide rate has tripled over the past three decades, and forty to fifty million Americans are on Prozac. "Mystery" afflictions for which there is no known cause—from chronic fatigue syndrome and fibromyalgia to False Memory Syndrome—torture millions, as do eating disorders, health-threatening obesity, and a host of other kinds of immiseration. A sterile, isolating, technologized society, truly pathological in its engulfing impoverishment.

Resist. Break ranks. Trust your desires. It's not you who's fucked up.

The cancer-like domination of technology and capital must be stopped and dismantled. After thirty years, a current of radical opposition is developing and it needs you.

The new movement is anarchy, which is about freedom, health, authenticity. Crossing the threshold into your adult years, how much freedom, health, and authenticity do you think the Megamachine will make possible for you? Does it not offer, instead, a "life" of mediation, hierarchy, and isolation on a dying planet?

We humans didn't always live like this. Our ancestors, who used fire to cook fibrous vegetables 1.7 million years ago, had a qualitatively different existence until just 10,000 years ago. Our adoption of agriculture brought division of labor and domestication. Until then, humans lived in keeping with an egalitarian ethos, with ample leisure time, gender equality, and no organized violence. Archeological studies in various parts of the world demonstrate this, our true history.

Unknown to most, this has been the mainstream view presented in anthropology and archeology textbooks for the past few decades. It sounds utopian, but it's now the generally accepted paradigm, and has had heartening implications for a growing number of us in the new culture of opposition. If we once—and for so long—lived in balance with nature and each other, we should be able to do so again. The catastrophe that's overtaking us has deep roots, but our previous state of natural anarchy reaches much further into our shared history.

Check out your life, as sold to you by this lying system. For you, and for all of us, we must break the spell of denial and reclaim our birthright. Come alive and fight!

John Zerzan

Jennifer Belle
Writer

Take Your Own Advice

In a way, my life has been one long focus group.

I have asked people for advice my entire life. I have never made a decision myself. I read my first self-help book in the fifth grade—*The Sensuous Woman* by J. I am convinced that my headaches, hives, excema, ulcer, carpal tunnel syndrome (severe, both arms), long bouts of vomiting that can only be stopped by a Compazine suppository, and a small brain tumor have all been the result of my inability to make the simplest of decisions.

I don't know why I ask everyone what to do. Perhaps it's a result of making so many bad decisions—dropping out of high school, dropping out of college to become an actress, quitting a lucrative job to become a full-time writer—all of which I regret. I don't trust myself.

Movie treatment: A MAN gets a book deal from Simon & Schuster to get famous WRITERS, most of whom no one has heard of, to write letters of ADVICE. The writers want more than the one hundred dollars he is willing to pay them, so he has to get a second job to give them more. He becomes obsessed with getting the writers to turn in their essays and sign their release forms, and as each essay finally arrives the disappointment of it starts to make him physically sick. The essays are stupid and weird. At best, pornographic. His phone bill skyrockets, his copying costs at Kinkos drain his bank account, his personal trainer (who he has hired in case he gets to go on Leno) has not only cost him every cent he has but has given him steroids, which will eventually give him cancer. Just when he thinks the book is finished, he remembers some other writer to approach. If only he can get a piece from so-and-schmo, the book will be okay, the project will be saved. But then the prized essay arrives scrawled on soiled toilet paper and signed by the famous writer and the MAN is thrust into despair again. Advice becomes an obsession, an addiction, and the cause for his ultimate demise. In the end, the quest for advice kills him.

I am like that man.

I asked everyone what advice to give.

James, the editor of this book, wanted me to write something "deeply romantic."

Another writer in the book suggested I "go to a bookstore and look at books of essays." He said the goal is just to "write something you're not embarrassed by."

My mother thought I should write advice about "being depressed."

That is the type of advice people give. Arbitrary. Unhelpful. Misleading.

For instance, this morning I got an invitation to an ex-friend's wedding. She is marrying a man I told her she was really wasting her time with. "He doesn't like you," I told her over a year ago. "Forget it. You're making a fool of yourself. He's not interested."

About a year ago, I was sitting in Caffe Reggio with a friend of mine after I had just found out I was pregnant. I'd only been dating my boyfriend for three months. As a full-time writer, I of course wanted the baby, just to give me something to do all day. I felt unbelievably sick and I wasn't sure if

Jennifer "I *am* the next generation" Belle, age 22, onstage at La MaMa, NYC.
Photo by Ira Cohen, 1990

Jennifer Belle

it was from the pregnancy or from having to decide whether or not to keep the baby. My morning sickness lasted all day and all night.

"You can do it," my friend said.

"How do you know?" I asked.

"You have more than enough closet space. You should have the baby."

My father, who ironically is a philosopher specializing in the abortion debate, thought I should have an abortion. "Why?" I asked, waiting for his expert opinion. He had written a whole book on the subject. "Because," he said, "if you have the baby and you break up with Andy you'll never get another man." My brother, independently, came up with exactly the same line of reasoning.

Their response took me by surprise. I had thought of and received many reasons for having an abortion, but never getting another man wasn't one of them. But what kind of person asks her *father* if she should have an abortion? My advice-getting was out of control. I had lost my integrity.

I was telling my friend I was leaning toward having an abortion when I noticed an old woman a few tables away from us shake her head disapprovingly. Every time I said something, I saw her shake her head at me. At first I appreciated her concern. It was comforting that she saw the seriousness of my dilemma. But soon I realized she was violently against the idea of abortion. I already felt terrible for what I was about to do. She didn't have to make me feel worse by putting her two cents in.

The woman kept shaking her head at me. It was one thing to get advice from friends but it was another to have a total stranger telling me what to do. Why didn't I just survey the whole neighborhood? Stand out on the street with a clipboard and explain to everyone individually the facts of my situation and ask them to check off "keep" or "terminate." If they check "keep" I could ask them to suggest a few names, because I'm sure that too would have to be a big committee decision.

"I don't think I should have the baby," I told my friend.

The old woman shook her head.

Finally, after she had shaken her head at me long enough, I decided to put a stop to it. I stood and stormed over to her table. "Stop shaking your head at me. I hate this as much as you do. Do you think I want to have an abortion? You should mind your own damn business, lady. Who are you to judge?" I yelled.

"I don't know what you're talking about," the old woman said. She looked shocked. "My head shakes because I have Parkinson's disease," she said.

I left the café and found a man on the street selling little toy dogs, their heads wobbling on springs, nodding yes and shaking no. I bought one and put it on my bedside table so its velveteen shaking head can always remind me to do what I want to.

I asked a few people what they thought of this essay and if they thought I should submit it or not.

"It's not about anything," one person said.

"The Parkinson's thing is just a cheap gag that you're using as a bridge to your own self-loathing," another person said.

"I don't like the movie treatment. It's gimmicky," another person said. "And I think you handle the topic of your abortion much too glibly. It's inappropriate. It makes you seem unthoughtful."

"Okay, okay," I said. "I'll lose the movie treatment and I'll take the abortion out."

The only thing worse than a person who asks advice is a person who gives it. There's a crazy girl who goes to the Caffe Reggio every day. She always says hello to me and I smile at her. Some of the waiters, my friends, won't even wait on her, she's so crazy. I'm the only one who's nice to her. Then yesterday she took a jar of jewelry cleaner out of a Duane Reade drugstore bag and opened it on the marble café table. She looked down at the tiny above-ground pool of blue liquid and swirled the little jewelry tray around. I wondered if she was so crazy she was going to start cleaning her jewelry right there in the café.

Jennifer Belle

When she thought no one was looking she dipped her teaspoon into the blue jewelry cleaner and tasted it cautiously, like medicine. Then she poured about half of the jar of jewelry cleaner into the teapot, poured herself a cup, and drank it down.

I felt some advice was in order. I leaned over toward her. "Don't do that," I said.

She glared at me, betrayed. "Don't worry about it, it's fine," she said. She stood and carried the Duane Reade bag with the rest of the jewelry cleaner in it into the ladies room and locked the door. I knew she was behind that green door with its faded Edgar Allen Poe quote, drinking down that soapy liquid. There was nothing I could do. I shouldn't have butted in. She never said hello to me again.

Sometimes a person doesn't want advice. That's why it's never a good idea to give it. People feel judged. People resent it even if they asked for it, the way they resent someone who has lent them money.

Recently on my book tour I visited my ex-boyfriend in Portland, Oregon. "Do you realize you've given me nothing but advice about every aspect of my life since you've been here?" he said bitterly when he took me to the airport. In his case I couldn't help it. Every aspect of his life was in shambles and when he told me he was thinking of getting one of those Japanese robot dogs instead of a real pet, how could I contain myself? Killing time in the airport, we went into a gift shop for pets so I could buy something for my real dog. He wanted to buy a statue of a giant blue cat meditating in the lotus position for his apartment. It was one of the most absurd things I had ever seen. I had to talk him out of paying $60 for it. Some people, like the crazy girl at Caffe Reggio and my ex-boyfriend in Portland, are just asking for it.

Vera Countess von Lehndorff (a.k.a. Veruschka)
Model, artist

Life Is an Adventurous Journey

Be awake! Try to notice as much as possible, even details. Observe yourself and others. Observe your habits, the way you walk and talk, your emotions, thoughts, and the way people live.

Aim far and be courageous, but examine your motives. You want to be the greatest? You want to just feed your ego? That's not so great.

Prepare yourself for the journey by strengthening mind and body. Don't waste precious time in meaningless ecstasies through hard drugs and excessive alcohol use. These substances fool us with fake happiness, but most times leave us with delusions, confusions, depression, loneliness, mental poverty, and no penny in the pocket!

As soon as possible, find out where your talents lie, then seek the best education and training. Believe in yourself and be determined in all activities as you strive for your accomplishments. Do not give in to despair in your weak moments or when you feel discouraged.

Good friends are worth more than megabucks. Value and build friendships.

You *can* experience the power to change yourself. Understand causality, meaning that whatever you think and do now is connected to past thoughts, words, and actions. Also, what you think and do now will sow the seeds for your future.

Remember that everything is impermanent. Nothing that is around you, not even yourself, has any lasting existence and will eventually disappear. Only the infinite clear space of mind is lasting, therefore train your mind to hold onto nothing. But fear not: You will not suffer when you die, nor take anything with you.

Life is like a beautiful bubble floating on the wind. It can vanish any moment.

Be aware of your responsibility to change the future. The world as you inherit it is endangered by people's egoism, greed, and cruelty. If you do not act, the world will decline and there will be no place for your children to grow up in peace.

Find those who are like you in every race and color. Teach one another and get involved in useful actions, even if they are small.

Try to share what you have with others. Greedy ones suffer. Riches do not guarantee happiness.

Have a good sense of humor, especially about yourself.

Think about the way things are with an awakened mind.

Even Buddha once said, "Don't just believe, find out for yourself!"

Have compassion and be fearless to make this world a better place.

Transformable plush, circa 1972. The legendary Veruschka.
Photo © Francesco Scavullo, reprinted with permission

Joel-Peter Witkin
Artist, photographer

Your life is the life of the world. If your life is of love, the world will love. Anything less and the world will continue to bleed. Live to know the reason you were born, your purpose in life, what happens after death. Read the classic books and the sacred books. Read the lives of the saints of religion, art, and life.

Recently, I heard a story of two men who worked carrying stones. One of the men was asked what he was doing. He replied, "I carry stones." When asked the same question, the other replied, "I'm building a Cathedral."

Baby-faced Joel-Peter Witkin, age 20.

Hakim Bey
Philosopher

Travel Advisory

Only in one area of human activity have I ever achieved what I'd call a modicum of real ability. So there's only one thing I feel competent to advise on: travel.

Since the 1960s I've traveled or lived in Morocco, Tunisia, Turkey, Iran, Afghanistan, Pakistan, India, Indonesia, Thailand, Taiwan, and the Philippines, plus a good deal of Western Europe and a bit of Eastern Europe at various times, and most recently and frequently, Ireland. The Persian poet Saadi said, "A jewel that never leaves the mine is never polished." Great slogan for travelers—although he might've added that the process (of having crap knocked off so as to shine) may well prove more painful to a human than to a rock.

The tourist is a traveler who avoids pain. A real traveler (in my jargon anyway) accepts pain if necessary to attain a goal, and is willing to spend a very long time at it.

If everything in the world has been leveled to the same flat plane of sameness by global capital, why bother to travel? What goal could be worth the pain?

My serious answer to this serious question would be that something else must've existed and might still exist. It's corrupt and generally dying. Even at its best it was badly flawed. But—it seems to me that it was also human. The glorious future we now inhabit here in the included zones is of course perfect, as we know. But it also strikes me as inhuman.

The dying corrupt thing I referred to can be called tradition, I suppose, though that's not a very good word for it. I wouldn't want to dignify it or denigrate it by such a term. Let's just say it's . . . something else. If that suffices, read on. If not, then this advice is not meant for you. The whole notion of "difference" or "the Other" has become too constricted and contentious. If I allow myself a certain romanticism of travel it's because I found in the Orient a certain *oriental romanticism* (however decayed) that required, let's say, an observer. A guest.

Being a guest can put a lot of strain on the traveler: harder work than being a host. Real hospitality is rare enough. A talented guest is a phoenix's egg. I'm not one so I had to work at it. When it got too difficult I'd rent a cheap hotel room for a week or so and hole up with a few books.

(You can only take a very few books with you. If you know where you're going and what you're going to find, take one or two basic factual works on the place and the subject of interest. Long, difficult books—in small print—are the best. In India there were always English paperbacks for a rupee. As we read them, we'd use them for toilet paper.) The late A. Ginsberg, a talented traveler, said in his *India Journals* that the ideal number of road companions is three: one to buy the tickets, one to find tea, and one to guard the luggage. Traveling alone can prove lonely and even dangerous, but also sometimes makes it easier to meet people. A matter of luck and temperament. In any case, don't wait for your friends to make up their minds. Go now.

If I were willing to face the miseries of the former Third World again, I'd go to Central Asia. I'd leave from Vienna and start the trip from Bukhara and Samarkand, through all the ex-Soviet "stans," then to Chinese Turkestan and the Taklamakan Desert, then to Tuva, the Altai region, and southern Siberia, then Mongolia and Manchuria. This area of the world was out-of-bounds in the '60s and '70s and '80s and '90s, and may soon be again. Bad religion, oil, natural gas, Soviet ruination—the window of opportunity could slam at any minute.

In general I'd take an interest in what used to be called the "Fourth" World. The term no longer seems applicable now that the multiplicity of "worlds" has been subsumed into the ecstasy of the free market. We should perhaps speak of *excluded zones*. Here the last resistances against enclosure are still being carried out: last enclaves of the "wild and primitive"; last vestiges of pre-futurity. These places may constitute a kind of avant-garde or conceptual outside, spearheading and embodying the only possible Other to the sameness of the same. Or maybe not. Either way, if I were thirsting for adventure and willing to dare disillusionment, I'd head for the extreme Arctic, perhaps, or the last jungles.

I find I travel best when I have a project. The project could be "Aimless Wandering," but that in itself is terribly difficult and I achieved it only rarely. Having a project means people to meet, places to go, mysteries to unravel. It provides you with a *persona*, which allows people to think they understand you. I for example enjoy scholarly antiquarian mystical subjects, so I tend to visit scholarly organizations, temples, shrines, and tombs. There I usually meet pleasant and informative people. I often thought that traveling in carpets, perfumes, semi-precious stones, or other old–fashioned merchandise would be a good way to meet people and get involved in situations. In any case one should be honestly passionate about the project, whether cultural, political, linguistic, psychedelic, erotic, etc. The tourist has no passion and everyone senses this immediately. So the tourist has no adventures.

Luggage: Don't take a backpack, please. The backpack marks you out for scorn. However, remember that sooner or later you'll have to walk a long way (in bad weather of some sort) with your luggage. Try dark-colored shoulder bags with adjustable straps, no sharp edges, and a lock. Clothes: Take one good outfit suitable for, say, dining with diplomats. Take warm clothes, light as possible, but not shiny poison-colored anoraks. Never wear shorts. Women who travel in Islamic countries should consider the cleverness of adopting the veil or something like it, since in this way they can enter the mysterious world of women, which men can't. In any case, men or women whose dress offends can expect to be treated badly, so why do it? It's stupid. If you adopt local attire, make sure it's "correct" for you (i.e., don't dress as a khan or a sweeper—unless you want to try to function as a khan or a sweeper). Local traditional fashion is designed for local climate, and no one will despise you for enjoying it (or if they do, they're the wrong people anyway).

"Adventure" usually means being lost, sick, out of your mind, and stuck somewhere without toilet paper, or in the middle of a war. Later on, around the old campfire, you can tell a ripping yarn—but while it's happening it's often terrifying. Of course there may occur adventures like, say, initiation, or a love affair, which (with luck) needn't prove too horrible. But you can't count on them. You can, however, count on getting sick. I almost never took a medicine kit along, and often had cause to regret it. In really outback places you need medicine for the locals.

Get calling cards printed. List your degrees and your profession. Don't hesitate to pass them out to anyone even barely literate or official. Never call yourself a journalist unless you have to. Try not to get stuck teaching English as a Foreign Language. Don't try to pretend you're not American (or British or whatever) because people aren't all stupid. Once I saw an American hippy almost stabbed in Peshawar because he thought he could make himself more popular by claiming to be German.

One of the best travelers I know says her secret is never to go anywhere covered by the Rough Guides. Good guidebooks are often banned in the countries they describe. But really there's no such thing as a good guidebook. You need them at first, but should try to transcend them.

When I'm traveling I usually avoid travel books, which are full of other peoples' subjective opinions. I especially dislike all negative travel writing (of the *Video Night in Kathmandu* school) as much as I hate to hear some depressing jerk describe a whole country or people in terms of insult and scorn. Those who give a bad report of a place simply reveal their own failures of attention and imagination. All such "warnings" are bogus. Listen to travelers' gossip for an occasional *good* tip or *happy* adventure; these may be worth something. Likewise with books.

Hakim Bey

Money isn't the only key to travel. I've met people who traveled without money at all—the really great travelers, actually. In a pinch you can always smuggle something. Don't say you can't afford it. You can even teach English if necessary. Don't put it off. Go now.

Diane Wakowski
Poet

Try to balance the material world and the idealistic one, so that your standards always remain high but you learn to gracefully accept and be second best. The all-or-nothing philosophy that dominates American culture is punishing and yields a shoddy civilization. You should never stop writing as if you could win the Pulitzer prize for excellence, and never stop competing as if you could be in the major leagues; you should never give up on finding the perfect love or being as beautiful as Elizabeth Taylor. But most of us are born without greatness, and if we can learn to be second best (or third, or even undistinguished) with grace—that is, with the same dedication, hard work, and discipline we would apply to being first—then the results would make a very fine civilization indeed.

This next piece of advice might be related to the first, but only in effect: Pay homage to your elders and peers whose writing you love or admire. Let other writers know how much you are in debt to them and how appreciative you are of their work by telling them, teaching their work well (if you teach), and by writing insightful critical articles about their work if you have those skills. Be generous; it will make you a better person and the world a better place to live in.

Natural poet: Diane Wakowski, late 1960s.

Jonathan Ames
Writer, performer

Jonathan Ames's Advice for People in Their Twenties

(This advice will be dispensed in categories to make things easy. And the conceit of all this, I guess, is that perhaps you'll benefit in some way. I hope so. Humans do learn from other humans, perhaps even from a human like me, so I'll proceed with that ideal in mind.)

On Heterosexual Sex
For the males, I recommend that you perform lots of oral sex, and I don't want to hear any protests or whining. Get down there! It's fun! It's delicious! It's sexy! And the benefits are enormous. Let's say you have problems with premature ejaculation, which many men in their twenties do suffer from. Well, if you go down on your lady-friend for a good fifteen to twenty minutes before attempting inter-course and then you only last forty-five seconds after penetrating, you have money in the bank because you were down there earlier lapping away like a prince. See what I mean? The girl won't be nearly as upset about premature ejaculation if you were selflessly licking her. And if you can make her come before failing at inter-course, all the better, though not all women come from oral sex (but a great many do). Also, by frequently eating out your girlfriend you will win your way to her heart. Women love men who go down there and who go down there with passion. They think you're worldly, giving, and highly attracted to them. Now, none of these things may be true, but it's good to give the appearance of all of them, especially if you want the girl to be crazy about you. And the main thing is that women derive a lot of pleasure from having their pussies licked—so give that to them!

I am not blind to the fact that some of you may have hang-ups about eating pussy. Sometimes, I admit, there is a strong odor of urine, though not always. But who knows what we must smell like in the crotch area, so don't be judgmental. Also, more often than not the bouquet down there is the greatest perfume known to man. But what I do recommend if there *is* an odor problem is that you breathe through your mouth—it's the perfect solution. This way you can lap and suck away at her for long periods of time. I have been in quite a few several-year-long relationships using this method.

What else can I tell you men? Be tender to your girls, but also don't worry about being a little rough in a sexy way: (1) Hold their arms over their heads during intercourse; (2) mix up short, gentle, teasing strokes with powerful, lusty, repeated thrusts (bang away, so to speak); and (3) praise and smack their behinds. I advocate this sort of roughhousing, because re-creating the relations that men and women enjoyed in caves several thousand years ago is usually a good thing for the bedroom. After all, what is a bedroom but a modern cave? Also, let me repeat: When you smack a woman's behind, PRAISE IT. Most women are insecure about their ass, so tell them that it is gorgeous. If it isn't, say so anyway. Most good relationships have several lies at their foundation.

For the women—thinking back to my pussy-eating advice for the men—I advocate parsing out your blowjobs. Don't let the guy get too used to them. He may get lazy and just want that after a while. So keep the blowjob as a special treat, unless you get into 69s, which are a good way to insure that your pussy is attended to (see above). My main advice to you, though, is to praise your boyfriend's penis. Tell him that it's just the right size or that it's big or that it's pretty. Anything. You'll make him feel really special and increase your chances of holding onto him. If you think his penis is ugly, but you still love him, then lie (see above). It's better to lie than not to say anything.

For men *and* women: If you live with someone, I recommend that every six weeks or so you don't sleep in the same bed for several nights. I once read in an Eastern sex book that it's healthy to be apart once in a while to maintain your yin and yang attraction. If you're in bed together all the time then your opposing electrical energies, which make you want to rub against each other in the first place, will wear off, like magnets losing their magnetism. Follow?

On Homosexual Sex

I apologize, but I don't have much advice in this category, except that if you're a man and not attracted to men, but want to touch another person's penis, then I recommend the transgender community. There you can get a pretty girl with a penis, so it's a lot easier psychologically, and more palatable.

And if you're a woman and want to touch another woman's breast or do other things, female bisexuality is completely endorsed these days by Hollywood, so there shouldn't be a problem. Do keep in mind, though, that just because you have these impulses it doesn't mean that you still can't enjoy men (like older male writers, who can easily be contacted through the Internet).

And if you're gay of either gender, I advocate all of the things I recommended for the straight reader. Tell lies when you need to and attend to each other orally, though I do think that the gay community, perhaps by necessity, is ahead of the straight community when it comes to oral sex.

On Food and Health

If you want to lose weight, don't eat dairy products or sugar products. Also, these things will increase your risk for various diseases and bad skin, so really do try to stay away from them, though a piece of chocolate once in a while, especially when you're depressed, is okay. Try not to eat meat, or cut it down to a treat—once a week, let's say, like women parsing out blowjobs (see above). If you're constipated, I recommend drinking lots of water, eating organic fruit, and helping yourself out every now and then with a fiber supplement. And in general, just eat less—they say the less you eat, the longer you live. Now, a lot of us might not want to live a long time, because it's so difficult, but there's always the hope that at some point it gets easier. Therefore, eat less so that you might get to this easier point, and then it's probably fun to just be around for a long time and see how things change.

On Drinking and Drugs (Vice Advice)

This is a hard one. Some people can enjoy substances and not feel like they're killing themselves or wrecking their lives. Bastards! But if you feel like you're abused by substances, then don't feel embarrassed to get some help. It takes more courage to ask for help than not to ask for help. I happen to be a coward, but I wish I'd ask someone for help. See, this is the danger of writing advice stuff. Your own hypocrisy and lack of spine is revealed. How can I write this essay when I'm not willing to do the right thing myself?

Perhaps I need to find a book of advice aimed for people in their thirties and that will get me to save my life before it's too late. (If you're feeling empathy for me, and you're female and sweet and promiscuous, see what I wrote above about finding older male writers on the Internet.)

On Money

Try to pay your bills on time! With the amount of money I've paid just in late fees, I could go to Paris and sit in a café and look at beautiful people for at least two weeks! But because I'm fearful of bills and I procrastinate, I can never pay anything on time and I've wasted tons of money. So I'm beginning to see a trend in this advice-giving thing: Don't be like me!

Oh, one more thing. If you can help it, don't use credit cards. They may be worse for your health than cigarettes. The amount of anxiety that credit card debt causes is notoriously crippling.

On Your Parents

Unless they were really horrible to you—like the father out of *The Great Santini* or the mother in *Sybil*—then try to forgive them for anything weird they might have pulled and love them as best you can. Saint Francis has some good lines that apply: "It's better to forgive than be forgiven. It's better to understand than to be understood. It's better to love than to be loved."

I advocate this attitude toward one's parents, because you'll feel much better in the long run and they'll feel better, too. Life is too short to have our souls be eaten away with resentment.

On Contacting Older Writers and Acting Out Sexual Fantasies and Infatuations
I advocate this quite strongly, but let me first summarize what we've covered so far. In the preceding categories, I believe I have touched on life's basics: sex (which includes love, sort of), food, money, stimulants, and family (parents). I don't know what else there is. Oh, yes, religion. Praying when you are in a bad way is very good, even if you are an atheist or agnostic. I'm an agnostic, and I find prayer to be highly distracting when I'm in deep trouble. Also, praying while in a bathtub with most of your head under water is particularly effective.

What else have I forgotten? Exercise. Try to elevate your heart rate for twenty minutes three times a week (basketball is good for this and rowing machines are interesting, and if nothing else, walk rapidly around your neighborhood and look in people's windows as a way to get yourself through the twenty minutes without being bored). There's also art: If you want to be an artist, then you need to persevere like crazy. And why not, what else is there to do? Same thing with goals of any sort: Might as well pursue them. Then there's travel: Good. And staying home: Also good.

I think that's everything. So, finally, this brings me to the last category, the self-serving one, and directed, somewhat, to the young ladies in the audience. You're young and full of life. I'm in my thirties and of late have become very aware of dying. I'd like to touch your younger bodies and forget about things for a little while. If this sounds appealing (see the first paragraph of this essay), then write me a note. And if you're male, you can also write me a note. Like touching a young girl's body, I take great pleasure in correspondence. (I should mention that I also very much enjoy older women's bodies, should you, an older woman, be reading this book by accident.) So all you young men and women, if you want to write to an older, maladjusted writer who presumed to give you advice (none of which you should take seriously, except the stuff about dairy, sugar, fiber, and your parents), please feel free to contact me and we can begin a pen pal relationship. I'm often quite lonely since I haven't managed my own life too well, and so maybe you can help me. And that's the best advice I can give: Try to help other people. It's supposed to make you feel good.

Only mildly perverted: Jonathan Ames as enfant terrible.
Photo by Bruce Weber, courtesy of the author

Jonathan Ames

Joanna Scott
Writer

Stuffed Peppers (A Recipe for Beauty)

Ingredients:

6 green peppers
½ cup breadcrumbs
1 cup milk
1 onion
1 cup ground meat
1 tbsp. tomato paste
2 cups sauce
1 egg
an open mind
(additions noted below)

1. Preheat the broiler. Make something. Sell it. Save whatever money you have left after you've paid for your necessities. Buy a bus ticket. Take the bus from Seattle to Miami, or from New York City to Los Angeles. Stop at 3 A.M. in Reno. While the driver is getting a cup of coffee, play a slot machine. Lose. Run back to bus; jump in just before the driver closes the doors. Sink into your seat. After you catch your breath, glance at the passenger next to you. Fall in love.

2. Cut the tops off six green peppers, then get yourself to the village of Portovenere. Bring a friend, someone you've known for years. Walk up past San Pietro to the ruins at the top of the promontory. From the crumbling wall, watch the sun drop into the sea. Read Cioran aloud. Tell secrets. Find a fig tree, pluck some fresh figs, and eat them. At midnight climb into the ruined turret near the cemetery, spread out your sleeping bags, and fall asleep to the sound of your friend singing. Wake up in darkness. Climb down from the turret and wander through the cemetery. Talk to ghosts.

3. Linger in the lobby of the theater after listening to a performance of Berg's *Lyric Suite.* Smile mysteriously when someone you hardly know calls you sentimental. Go home in a subway car surrounded by people speaking a language you don't understand. Broil the peppers until they are blistered on all sides.

4. Ride a horse over a jump, soak yourself with water from a hose, read a newspaper, clench your fingers into a fist, walk in an unfamiliar place without opening a map, think about history, dodge cars, skip a stone across a fountain, watch a child run barefoot along a sidewalk, soak breadcrumbs in milk.

5. Having finally accepted the fact that someone you thought you wanted something to do with wants nothing to do with you, continue to cook dinner for family and friends. Fry onions with ground meat. Mix in tomato paste. Think about learning to swim. Think about the person you met on the bus in Reno. Think about a poem. When the phone rings, answer it.

6. After gently packing the meat into the peppers, sit with acquaintances at an overpriced outdoor café. Smoke a Gauloises. When talk turns to money, discreetly feed a pigeon pieces from the crust of your blackberry tart. Silently repeat to yourself the opening sentence of Beckett's *Molloy*.

7. Dip the top of each pepper in an egg. Sprinkle with crumbs. Go to work. Work hard. Sit with acquaintances at a tavern behind the factory where you've spent the day sweeping floors. When talk turns to race, listen carefully. If you disapprove, object. If someone threatens you with a knife, tell a joke. When everyone else is laughing, run.

8. Risk embarrassment.

9. Ignore no-trespassing signs and critics. Walk through instead of around. Don't become too attached to a favorite pen. Bake peppers until the tops are crisp.

10. Combine admiration, pride, curiosity, insight, grief, restlessness, desire, nostalgia, hope, pleasure, ambition, hilarity, jealousy, wonder, recklessness, affection, anger, hunger, luck, despair, caution, selfishness, and selflessness. Stir. Kiss. Spoon the sauce over the peppers and season to taste.

Great Scott: "It is in these moments that Nature becomes our Egeria."—Disraeli

Stewart Home
Writer

Defiant pose: Home is where the heart is. Age 19.

On the Misery of the Literary Life

I too was once young, and having reached middle age, I can see that I've learned much more from my own mistakes than from any guidance I was offered by my elders. This, of course, had as much to do with my extravagantly stubborn refusal to listen as with the rather obvious flaws in the counsels I received. Among the things that particularly irked me as I grew up were threats, wrapped in flattery, that were endlessly dispensed as if I were being offered sagacious advice. Throughout my teenage years, the constant refrain directed at me by stucco authority figures was that since I was obviously intelligent, if I'd just knuckle under I'd get on in life. In the minds of these sawdust Caesars, intelligence was the ability to understand that those who didn't bow down before the Great God of Authority drew a short straw in the "adult" world. I grew up in a time and a place where there was pretty much full employment, and the fact that by the age of seventeen I was happily claiming welfare became, for my former teachers, a shocking illustration of the fate of those who refuse to do what they are told. Thoroughly perplexed by the tedium of their own dull lives, these buffoons vainly imagined they could condemn me for lacking their humble ambitions, and for having no wish to hold down a regular job. I was interested in rather more grandiose projects, such as overthrowing capitalism and thereby transforming life on this planet into something that was actually worth living.

As a result of these teenage experiences, I'm not inclined to tell the young what to do. I have no advice to give, and instead simply offer stories from my life as parables, in the hope that they will at least raise the odd belly laugh. Of course, my teachers' claims that my innate intellectual abilities would enable me to get on in the capitalist economy were patently untrue—when I entered the employment market, I did so with the handicap of having attended a sink school. The ability to conform and having the "right" social background were much more easily assessed and rewarded than something as nebulous as "intelligence." Fortunately, I was able to turn this to my own advantage. The exams I'd passed at school without making any particular effort to do so meant I was overqualified for factory work. I did try laboring immediately after leaving school, since such employment was readily available to me if I played down my modest academic successes, but after a few months I concluded that breaking my back six days a week was too much like hard work.

To be entitled to welfare payments, I had to actively seek employment. My local job center would secure me interviews for low-grade clerical work, and I'd go along to these parlays smartly dressed in a black suit and white socks. When potential employers asked about my hobbies, I'd say I liked to read German philosophy and French literature. I'd blatantly lie about my ability to pursue these interests in the original languages. What I'd actually read were translations and these amounted to little more than a few dozen novels by the likes of Sartre and Robbe-Grillet, which I'd rounded out with some meagre scraps of Marx (at that time I hadn't even started on Hegel). I always made sure I did very well in interviews, so that potential employers would think I'd leave them the moment something more lucrative came up. Needless to say, while I was not surprised by my inability to secure a position, the welfare officers assigned to me were inordinately perplexed by my predicament.

I claimed welfare on and off for many years, and while doing this knocked out the odd book. Right from the start, I was aware of the misery of literary life, and I was simultaneously developing a critique of the notion of characterization within literature that demonstrated how it was inextricably linked to the thoroughly ossified and ideological chimera of "national character." I was interested in world culture and continuous becoming, and despised

literature since literature was always and already "national literature." As a consequence, I saw those men and wimmin who made up
the British literary establishment as legitimate targets for the odd
prank that contested the hegemony of their views. My hoaxing of
the camp that developed around *Satanic Verses* author Salman
Rushdie in the wake of the fatwa was considered to be among the
more obnoxious of my japes. Rushdie had written a book that was
considered blasphemous by certain Muslims, and the death threats
that a small number of those he'd offended made as a consequence
of his shenanigans became an international news story. In early
1994 I mailed the following fake press release to various literary
critics as a way of addressing issues raised by the Rushdie affair:

THE CONSORTIUM PRESENT SMASH THE FATWA, BURN THE KORAN! At a Secret Location in London, 14 February 1994.

Salman Rushdie has teamed up with conceptual artist
John Latham to create a protest piece on the fifth anniver-
sary of the death sentence issued against him by the Iranian
government.

Latham will be recreating one of his famous SKOOB tow-
ers of the 1960s, using copies of the Bible and the Koran.
Like its predecessors, this tower will be spectacularly burnt,
reducing the books to ashes. Skoob is, of course, books spelt
backwards.

Salman Rushdie says this collaboration demonstrates his
commitment to artistic experimentation and opposition to
censorship. "Since going into hiding, I've been studying Middle Eastern history and now realise that the workers are the
only people in a position to defy intransigent Islam," the
author explained. "In 1958, when Qasim and the free officers
seized power in Iraq, the workers killed the monarch and
burnt the Koran. This is the kind of activity my collaboration
with John Latham is designed to encourage."

Journalists wishing to attend this unique artistic event

are asked to ring Brian on 071 351 7561 by 10 February, so that they can be vetted prior to being issued with details of the redirection point.

The telephone number was that of Brian Stone, one of Rushdie's literary agents. This hoax caused a huge security flap costing thousands of pounds and for several days the Rushdie camp was left wondering whether my mailing was part of an international plot being orchestrated against the author.

All good pranks are done for a purpose, and I wanted to protest against a situation in which one was either supposed to be for Rushdie and free speech, or else one was allegedly a Muslim fundamentalist. I found the British press coverage of the Rushdie affair quite extraordinary; it treated Islam as if it were monolithic, whereas if Christianity had been presented in this way there would have been an outcry, since the differences between Catholic, Protestant, and Orthodox positions are readily apparent to white European journalists. By ignoring the very different forms Islam takes—for example, in its Shiite, Sunni, and Sufi guises—much of the British press coverage of the fatwa was unconsciously racist. This is something I'd hoped Rushdie would speak out against, since it is inconceivable that he hadn't grasped the ways in which his plight highlighted how art and culture—much more than pseudo-scientific justifications of bigotry—were the chief conduits of racism and ethnic absolutism toward the end of the twentieth century. I deliberately gave Rushdie political views to the left of those he actually held in the statement I made up for him, since this was what I'd have hoped he'd use the situation he found himself in to say. I wanted to demonstrate there were other positions to those being expounded upon in the British press.

When a *Big Issue* journalist put two and two together and fingered me as the man responsible for the Rushdie hoax, I was threatened with legal action and told I'd be shunned by the publishing industry. Apart from a story in *The Big Issue* (#65, 8–14 February

1994) at the time I played this prank, it went unreported in both the British and the international press. Due to government cuts that made it increasingly difficult to claim unemployment benefits, I came off welfare shortly after I pulled the Rushdie prank, and I've made a living from my writing ever since. Contrary to various people's expectations—not least my own—the literary establishment has embraced rather than shunned me. This does not, of course, prevent me from criticizing it, and exploring the ramifications of this and similar examples of repressive desublimation as I do so.

I was surprized when in June 2001 I won an Arts Council of England Writers' Award and Salman Rushdie, who was presenting the prizes, gave me mine without so much as addressing a single word to me about my prank, since he knows who I am and what I'd done. Prior to Rushdie handing out the prizes, he made a speech. At the end of his pep talk about the importance of writing, the microphone was appropriated by an MC, so there was no opportunity for me or any of the other prizewinners to make use of it to raise political and cultural issues. I went along to the ceremony hoping to question Rushdie about the cultural racism that had been mobilized around opposition to the fatwa against him, but the event was orchestrated in such a way that I was unable to talk to him about why, to the best of my knowledge, he'd never publicly challenged the bigotry of some of his supporters. The fact that I consider Rushdie to be a mediocre novelist does not necessarily mean that I must also hold a low opinion of him as a person, but I have to confess that I was unimpressed by the fact that while he was prepared to shake my hand, he said nothing to me whatsoever, not even "congratulations." Those who make half a (counter-)revolution only dig their own graves.

John Rechy
Writer

Advice? The only good advice is the kind you give to yourself, too late; that is, from the vantage of years, you look back on who you were and you wish you had been able to have a blunt talk with yourself that would have helped you avoid what you regret, events that pursue you in judgment, times when you may have added to the world's overload of unkindness, of cruelty. But then, without having gone through those tur-

The ageless John "Don't fuck with a legend" Rechy.

bulences, you wouldn't be the person who would be able to look back like that. So: Advice? Somewhat worthless, finally.

Still—

If you're creative, don't squander your talent. It's the blessing of blessings, the one substitute for salvation. If you're an artist, remember that what is written—or painted, or filmed, or composed, etc.—is all that never changes, never dies (if one is lucky enough to get one's work published, shown, performed). In literature, Catherine and Heathcliff will forever search for each other, Buck Mulligan will forever be coming down a stairway to greet Stephen Daedalus, and Molly Bloom will forever be ruminating in bed. That, then, is the only way to stop time.

This, too—not advice, but observations based on one's own view: One should live like the star of one's life, and lead one's life as if it were a grand novel, a grand film. I'll stick to the imagery of film for ready references and examples. Many people live their lives as if they are featured players in others' stories; others surrender to being featured players, or supporting actors, actresses; still others disappear into the crowds as bit players; many become only walk-ons in others' lives. Be the star.

Always look as if you're going to be photographed; dress consistent with your starring role—self-conscious elegance, self-conscious disarray, depending on the context. Always be conscious of yourself. Talk like the star of your life and give yourself quotable dialogue; walk like the star of your life, turning action into choreography. Never put yourself down—others are too eager to. Praise yourself deservedly, but make certain you deserve the praise.

Don't listen to advice. Except this: Don't add to the vast cruelty in the world. And: Be creative.

Larry Niven
Writer

Niven's Laws

To the best I've been able to tell in fifty years of observation, this is how the universe works. I hope I didn't leave anything out.

1a. Never throw shit at an armed man.

1b. Never stand next to someone who is throwing shit at an armed man. You wouldn't think anyone would need to be told this. Does anyone remember the Democratic National Convention of 1968?

2. Never fire a laser at a mirror.

3. Mother Nature doesn't care if you're having fun. (Please note: You will not be stopped! There are things you can't do because your metabolism uses oxidation of sugar, or you're made of meat, or you're a mammal, or human. Funny chemicals will kill you slow or quick, or ruin your brain . . . or prolong your life, if you're careful. You can't fly like an eagle, nor yet like Daedalus, but you can fly with a hang glider, or ride through the sky in something like a cramped living room. There are even answers to jet lag. You can cheat. Nature doesn't care, but don't get caught.)

4. $F \times S = k$. The product of Freedom and Security is a constant. To gain more freedom of thought and/or action, you must give up some security, and vice versa. These remarks apply to individuals, nations, and civilizations. Notice that the constant k is different for every civilization and different for every individual.

5. Psi powers, if real, are nearly useless. Over the lifetime of the human species we would otherwise have done something with them.

6. It is easier to destroy than to create. If human beings didn't have a strong preference for creation, nothing would get built.

7. Any damn fool can predict the past. Generals are famous for this, and certain writers too.

8. History never repeats itself.

9. Ethics changes with technology.

10. Anarchy is the least stable of social structures. It falls apart at a touch.

11. There is a time and a place for tact. (And there are times when tact is entirely misplaced.)

12. The ways of being human are bounded but infinite.

13. The world's dullest subjects, in order:

    a. Somebody else's diet

    b. How to make money for a worthy cause.

    c. Special-Interest Liberation.

14. The only universal message in science fiction: There exist minds that think as well as you do, but differently. Niven's corollary: The gene-tampered turkey you're talking to need not be one of them.

15. Niven's Law for Musicians: If the applause wasn't louder than the music, something's wrong. Play better or softer.

16. Fuzzy Pink Niven's Law: Never waste calories. Potato chips, candy, or hot fudge sundae consumption may involve you, your doctor, your wardrobe, and other factors. But Fuzzy Pink's Law implies:

> Don't eat soggy potato chips.
> Or cheap candy.
> Or an inferior hot fudge sundae.
> Or a cold soggy pizza.

17. There is no cause so right that one cannot find a fool following it. This one's worth noticing. At the first High Frontier Convention, the minds assembled were among the best in the world, and I couldn't find a conversation that didn't teach me something. But the only newspersons I ran across were interviewing the only handicapped person among us. To prove a point, one may seek out a foolish communist, thirteenth-century liberal, Scientologist, High

Frontier advocate, Mensa member, science fiction fan, gamer, Christian, or fanatical devotee of Special-Interest Lib—but that doesn't really reflect on the cause itself. *Ad hominem* arguments save time, but it's still a fallacy.

18. **No technique works if it isn't used.** If that sounds simplistic, look at some specifics: Telling friends about your diet won't make you thin. Buying a diet cookbook won't either. Even reading the recipes won't do it. Knowing about Alcoholics Anonymous, looking up the phone number, even jotting it on real paper, won't make you sober. Buying weights doesn't give you muscles. Signing a piece of paper won't make missiles disappear, even if you make lots of copies and tell every anchorperson on earth. Endlessly studying designs for spacecraft won't put anything into orbit. And so forth. But you surely know someone who tried it that way, and maybe you're one yourself.

19. **Not responsible for advice not taken.**

NIVEN'S LAWS FOR WRITERS

1. **Writers who write for other writers should write letters.**

2. **Never be embarrassed or ashamed by anything you choose to write.** (Think of this *before* you send it to a market.)

3. **Stories to end all stories on a given topic, don't.**

4. **It is a sin to waste the reader's time.**

5. **If you've nothing to say, say it any way you like.** Stylistic innovations, contorted story lines or none, exotic or genderless pronouns, internal inconsistencies: Feel free. **If what you have to say is important and/or difficult to follow, use the simplest language possible.** If the reader doesn't get it then, it's not your fault.

6. **Everybody talks first draft.** Don't react till you know what he meant.

Maxx Aardman
Poet

Kindly Keep Your Tongues in Your Trousers Until You Have Something to Say

My name is Maxx Aardman and I wrote *The Maxx Factor: Poems*, which is why I'm here. As a guy I'll talk about bodily functions (sex) and language mainly to the guys. A sample poem:

> VICE VERSE
> Tight stuff—
> that squeezes the bullshit out
> but leaves the gut.

The MF hasn't come out yet, which is why you haven't heard of it before. But then you haven't come out either, or why would you be reading a book of advice?

My advice to you is, "Know words." My surname, for instance, means "earth-man," an enviable condition if you're a pig—in which case you'd be a vark, as in aard-vark. (You guessed it, "earth-pig." See how easy it's going to be? "Where's the sex?" you ask. Hey, don't be a vark!)

My advice is, know words in the biblical sense ("In the beginning was the word. . . ."). That means getting in touch with words. Once you're in touch with words you can be in touch with anything, anyone, at one remove. But then to begin the beguine, press the flesh, or advance to Tango you'll first have to remove the remove, right? For instance, if you want to party down with some rippling bit of poetry-in-motion you spot trolling the avenue, have some language handy. Until you toss out a line you can't set the hook and she's not going to let you pull up alongside, much less try to board her. Money certainly won't do it, or fame, or looks. (Just kidding; don't panic.) Even mere styling might get her attention, but then to hold onto it will take . . . words. The right words, not the left.

So don't be *gauche* or *sinister*. Be self-assured, *adroit*.

So what's up with all the italics? Just my point. Until you know the tools you can't do the job. Or as Philotexas once put it, "If all you got born in life with is a silver hammer in your mouth, you'll want to screw everything in sight up." (Maybe what he meant was, "A man who only has a hammer will fix everything with a nail.") If all you have by way of love-lures is, "Hey, bay-bee, I seen you around somewhere or what? And, hey, that a stud-finder you wearing around your neck or what?" then, hey, she better remember seeing you around and she better have a stud-finder hanging, or she'll keep right on trolling for fresher, more righteous fish. Or what.

In this life, with these wonders we call women, you're going to need to get down on your knees and scratch—at the earth, the dirt, the matrix concealing the goods, the goods that really matter. Know words and begin to know the world; know the world and the world will make you known, then others will want to know you. Just as she will—if you know what to say, how, when. And when to mean it. But how are you going to mean it if you don't know what the words you use are made of? You don't want to end up like that guy—isn't that Philotexas again?—there on the sports bar screen assuring us he recognizes the importance of "bondage" when it comes to keeping families together, do you?

So take those words I just italicized. You know what *gauche* means, in public. And *sinister*. But do you know them intimately, with their clothes off—the veils of a hundred, a thousand years, almost two thousand, lifted away? Both words are rooted in terms for left-handedness and mean, respectively, "ill-mannered" and "seeming evil." What, you may well wonder, do such things have to do with bodily functions or which hand you use?

Rewind another thousand years or so, to when Judaic people (later Judeo-Christians, then plain Christians, then Catholics, Protestants, Mormons, and finally the NRA) lived in tribes unified by sacred rites, life-or-death rites deliberately performed with the right hand. The right hand could not be defiled without calling down a curse on yourself, your family, your clan or tribe. And while defiling could mean many things—killing, stealing—most often it meant one: masturbation. In a time when the fruits born of the dictum "Go forth and multiply" were laborers and warriors whose sheer numbers determined the future welfare of the nation, it was a serious no-no to spill the stuff of future citizens into Onan's sand trap. But, if you were in, let's say, a medical emergency, and the right gal hadn't caught your fancy or fancied your pitch, you'd damned well better heal yourself with the left hand, keeping the right hand "clean."

So maybe some *jeune fille* with a heavenly smile adorned by irresistible piercings reviles you for being *gauche*, for coming on *sinister*, knowing in her heart of hearts, from a glance or a sniff, that you, good buddy, are too readily self-satisfied to suit her tastes. On the other hand, so to speak, she might think you're *adroit* (which signifies—you guessed it—literally "right-handed" and figuratively just plain "right," as in "Mr. Right"), meaning she believes you're skillful with your hands, *cunning* with your mind and *tongue*.

It won't overtax even the poorest imagination to guess where "cunning" originates. Those who lack physical strength—such as women before Jane Fonda (who with her Buns of Steel turned Ted) or Hillary Rodham (who with her pre-congressional grin [check the derivation of *congress*] drove Slick Willy to extramarital chips and dip)—must, of necessity, approach problems less directly than do their testosterone-toughened brethren; their ways, a.k.a. "wiles," are carefully concealed so they cannot be easily thwarted. Their bodies conceal a primary organ with which *cunning* shares a cognate, which is *Kunda*, an ancient great goddess of the Orient. Hence "Kundalini" yoga, "kind," "kin," "country" (i.e. mother-land), etc. You say you don't think all this really matters? I tell you even the word *matter* is implicated. It comes from the same word-root as *mother*, so think *maternal*. (Do consult Barbara Walker's *The Woman's*

Encyclopedia of Myths and Secrets, though you'll limp away with your inner barbarian much chagrined.)

A woman of experience (*experience* and *peril* share common ground, actually and etymologically) likes a man with quick wits and slow, sure hands for the same reasons a peahen fancies a peacock with a broad spangled fantail and sure balance. One *inspires* her *imagination,* the other assists in making it happen. She is enthused by such a one, who will surely *sympathize* with her desires. (*Inspiration:* breathing in the spirit [usually a god]; *imagination:* making a picture, or image, from the inspiration; *enthuse:* to take god in[to one's self]; *sympathize:* to suffer with.) You can see how the underpinnings of the language here serve to elevate the script to a grander, more ancient kind of drama, a mating ritual really, a rite of passage from stranger to *lover.* (Stranger: one who, being foreign, doesn't know your ways or share your rites. As for *love,* you may already be aware that *Liebschen* [German for "beloved"] and *liberty* share the Latin root *liber,* meaning "free," especially as opposed to being enslaved. There is also a Latin god of growth named *Liber,* the likelihood for growth being most auspicious where the condition of freedom [i.e., love] prevails. [At this point, it may look like the divine *Libera*ce, that mid-century sequined Hollywood semaphore for self-love, is about to pop up here somewhere; he's not.])

Men—tending to depend too much on their brains (which despite frequent upgrades still require constant tweaking), too little on their hearts (born knowing everything worth knowing from the start)—are always playing catch-up with women. Despite all the spin-doctoring of recent decades, women are different from men. Women intuit early that their primary biological functions, which revolve around birthing as surely as planets revolve around the sun, are in equal parts secular and sacred business, the latter usually at an unspoken level so as not to spook the male. Being goddesses by virtue of their DNA, women want men who are gods; fortunately for us, their innate grace and humor (periodically reinforced by their blinding hormonal drives) result in a sensibility not readily deterred even by such dead giveaways as hand-painted trout ties, microbrewery label collections, or braidable body hair. So, while it may be true that girls just want to have fun, women just want to have men. (Unless, of course, like us, they prefer girls. That's a whole other ball game. Or, in Zen-speak, non-ball game.)

Men are boys precariously perched on the hairy shoulders of their forefathers, all important connections hardwired, all systems Go. *"Gnothi seauton,"* advised old Socrates: "Know thyself." Know also, added brother Darwin, that said sweet self is simply the latest in a succession of selves scampering back up into the trees and slithering on back down into the sea. What knits the first to the last is the conceptualizing capacity of language, the ongoing process of communal consciousness as it is raised from primal foundations to whatever futuristic penthouse we're glory-bound for next. Knowing language is knowing history via those telling snapshots taken by tongues every step of the way. Language evolves just as *Homo sapiens* evolves.

To know a word is not simply to understand its current usage; rather, it is to know at what point it is now passing in its continuous trajectory. Likewise, to know a woman is not merely to understand what she's about but to comprehend what she's becoming— then to *sympathize* with her, to *enthuse* and *inspire* her. To *love* her is indeed to *liberate* her.

There's more. John's "In the beginning was the Word" goes on: "and the Word was with God, and the Word was God." God, the term, is itself a sort of placeholder, an unutterable silence referring to something ultimately real but without meaning in itself. Many early peoples believed, as some still believe, that to speak the name of their God aloud was to defile it and even to risk losing contact with it; to identify God with a mortal word makes the infinite finite. Today, Orthodox Jews, when advertising holidays in newspapers, for instance, spell out J*hovah half-concealing His name. In the arena of pop culture, which we might not have expected to generate such marvels of introspection, Puff Daddy with his rapier wit had a similar take on the divine Jennifer Lopez, rechristening her J-Lo.

Yet even the most ancient terms for the Ultimate One— Jehovah, Yahweh, etc.—were epithets with earlier demotic meanings, familiar enough to early scholars, largely neglected, concealed, and ultimately forgotten by those who've followed. Why? Because those divine epithets, which have reached us only after being monkishly translated into such ill-focused euphemisms as "creative force" or "heavenly father," at first were far earthier in their associations and had such honorific (and at the time inoffensive) referents as "phallus," "cosmic phallus," "erect-phallus-in-the-sky" (see Allen Edwardes' *Erotica Judaica*). Is it a man, is it a bird? No—it's . . . Phallus, the most potent image for men faced with cosmic cunning. A bit self-glorifying, isn't it? you may ask, all this making of God in the image of man? Or rather, manhood. Well there's a history of that in the Romance languages. Consider the *vir* in *virtue*, which derives from the Latin for man, as in *vir*ile or *vir*ulent. Literally speaking, unless you are a man, you cannot even possess virtue! Or so the Romance languages imply. Some romance.

Speaking of men and sex and epithets (fancy's names for things) and cunning and the veils of time that hide even as they reveal, "Adam" was an epithet before it was a proper name, and before it was proper it was improper. Cheesy dictionaries and entry-level scholars tell us Adam means "man" or "a man" or "the man." As with much "learning," more may be concealed thereby than is revealed. So go buy a better dictionary, consult a more *radical* etymologist (one who will pit himself against the risks of going to "the root"), and you might avoid going home with a headful of bland learning ("headpiece stuffed with straw" as T. S. Eliot put it). Depending how deeply you wish to dig, how many veils you lift, Adam means "man of earth" (sound familiar?); lifting another layer, "man of red earth"; and lifting yet another we discover "man of earth and blood mixed together." This is as far as the good Christian fathers will want you to go—but being so engaged you'll be wanting to go all the way by now, won't you? What you'll find is this: Adam means "man made of earth mixed with menstrual blood." What's startling is the implication that woman did not follow man but preceded him; indeed, she provided his building blocks, not vice versa. (See B. Walker, *ibid*.) And what a ribbing we chromosomal by-products will be in for once news of this gets out.

So there we have it, a prime example of how a word may be co-opted from an older, earthier, more *mater*ialistically mystical and *mater*nal religion. In this case it comes from the era of the Great Goddess, when it was believed that man sprang not from clay and the breath (or spirit—remember *inspiration*) of God, but rather from earth-matter (*mater* = mother) mixed with woman's wise blood. So if hu*man*(sic)ity has an altogether womanly origin— female being original, male derivative—it may be true after all, guys, that collectively we're just some sidestreet, back alley, or abandoned parking lot at the old Rocket Drive-In in Gene Village.

Fast-forward now to the irreverent present, when "the word was God" can be radically rendered (word = language = *lingua* = tongue) this way: "the tongue was [like] the phallus." Heady stuff—a simile to put a smile on the stone lips of Mt. Rushmore. Yet we find in Sanskrit an equation similar to this one in Latin and Hebrew. The *lingam* is a tall slender stone still ritually erected and revered in villages throughout India, where it is worshiped as a source of divine regenerative power. It is a phallus, tongue-like in configuration, and it is often counterpointed by a *yoni,* the female organ represented by a circular stone with a hollow center, revered as a creative source older than the *lingam.* The ritual union of these symbols through intercourse represents, in the West as in the East, a reunion devoutly to be desired. Called *hieros gamos* in Greece, that union was the sacred marriage enabling two primal fragments to enjoy original wholeness. It still is.

The mantra best-known in the United States is *Om mani padme om*, literally stating "the jewel is in the lotus" and symbolically meaning that the *lingam* is in the *yoni* or (westward ho for the Judeo-Christian equivalent) "God[male]'s in his heaven[female]— all's right with the world." *Hieros gamos,* in deep disguise. And how appalled Mr. Browning and his readers would be if they'd realized what his proper English translates from—or into. And yet this is, after all, the same Robert Browning who once, unwittingly, used "twat" in a poem while under the impression it was an archaic name for "hat," having discovered that tangy term in a poem rather bawdier than he realized, wherein a priest pulled a nun's twat down over his head.

To mean what you say you've got to know what your words mean, as well as what you mean. It's that simple. Neither words nor women are dull if you know how to approach them—or boring if you know how to let them *educate* you. (Educate, after all, means "to be led on or out.") And so, my young friends, we've come full circle.

Know yourself, of course, as Socrates often said before being sentenced to death for corrupting the morals of the youth. And know words as you would know women: wholly, holy down to the last loophole howling out the ultimate Hallelujah from the burning bush itself.

And kindly keep your tongues in your trousers until you have something worth saying.

A mind, as the man said, is a terrible thing.

Enjoy, enjoy.

William T. Vollmann
Novelist

Every time is without precedent, every generation is the most novel ever, so it's hard to see why my advice should be any more timely than Plato's. Nonetheless, I'm always looking for advice myself. (In fact, my main grudge against psychotherapy, of which I was once an earnest consumer, is that people who are paid to listen but not to suggest are less effective helpers than friends who know you, care about you, and encourage you to act in some way.) Anyway, here's the free sermon you requested:

1. Know yourself. Know your limitations and don't transgress them; know your boundaries and don't let anyone else transgress them; be proud of your gender, color, and everything about you that doesn't hurt others gratuitously. If you are a whore or a junkie or a soldier and you've chosen to be, then be proud of it. If you can't be proud of what you are, be something else.

2. The President always lies. The high school principal always lies. The FBI always lies. The boss always lies. Whatever these people tell you, take it apart until you see their hidden interest.

3. Try to love as many people as you can (i.e., be proud of who *they* are—don't transgress *their* boundaries). Just for the hell of it, try to love someone as unlike you as possible.

4. Be proud of *where* you are. If the President of the oil company or the gang of wilding teenagers starts to fuck it up, then do something about it.

5. Be proud of your body and the bodies of others. Enjoy yourself.

6. Be proud of your country. Learn about its history. Know its limitations. Help it repeat its successes, not its mistakes.

7. Don't buy anything or use anything you don't need or want. Try to do constructive things with cash.

8. Encourage the legalization and licensing of prostitution, abortion, pornography, and non-addictive drugs. Just say yes.

9. Boycott television, lawyers, shopping malls, and other opiates of the masses.

10. Vote.

11. If you have money and want to travel, don't go to the Arctic, the Galapagos, and other sensitive areas that are being destroyed by people like you.

12. Try to stay where you are as long as you can, get to know your neighbors, and make the place as nice as you can.

13. Don't be afraid to die for what you believe in, but try not to kill others for it.

14. Learn to read as well as you can. Reading gives you access to information, which is freedom. Computer literacy is all very well and good, but paltry in comparison.

15. If the president can watch you, he will watch you.

16. Anyone can be an artist of sorts. At the very least, trying to create something beautiful will help you see beauty in other created things, and that will make you happy.

17. Work with your neighbors to stamp out gratuitous violence whenever possible. If someone stabs a person on the subway, everyone else ought to jump on him and immobilize him—if necessary by killing him.

18. If the president advises what to do, consider his advice. If the president orders you what to do, do the opposite.

19. Every day, remind yourself that you are no better or worse than anyone else in the world—even the president.

20. Ask yourself again how much you need vehicles and plastic in your life.

21. If you can't save the world in any other way, try your own private army.

P.S. No advice will do a damned bit of good.

Chris Kraus
Writer

Doomed Love

Dear James,

Thank you for the opportunity to speak to the "next generation" via your book. I take it from the *extremely* flattering tone of your letter we're not being paid. But that's okay. While I may not be one of the "smartest, most creative people on the planet" (James, it is a very big planet), I guess I *do* have something to say on the topic that you asked me to write on, which is obsession.

Julia Butterfly, eat your heart out. Chris Kraus, age 14.

James, I guess the reason you thought of me in relation to obsession (a word that's hard to divorce now from the name of the perfume) is that I wrote a book called *I Love Dick*, which was based on hundreds of letters. They were love letters to a person named "Dick." He was a famous theorist and critic I had a crush on. Was Dick an obsession? Well yeah, but only sort of. Because by writing to Dick, I found out I had an obsession for talking. "Dick" became "dick," and since I was (and still am) a straight girl, craving dick really meant craving someone to talk to.

Now, I gather from what you say in your letter, your book aims to be kind of intellectual. So it may be of interest to those in your target age-group—the twentysomethings outside the academic realm who "may not have benefited from the economic boom that was the '80s and '90s" (James, I didn't benefit much from it either, and if what you say—that you're working full-time as a waiter—is true, perhaps neither did you)—that this whole Dick adventure actually mirrored a project undertaken by the philosopher-poet Antonin Artaud when his poems were rejected from *Nouvelle Revue Francaise* by

Jacques Rivière, the magazine's editor. This happened in Paris some-time during the 1930s, when Artaud was a twentysomething too, though with the added cultural advantage of being crazy. When Artaud received Jacques Rivière's tepid form rejection letter, he wrote him back—not challenging Rivière's ultimate decision, but drawing him out, engaging him personally, probing for more infor-mation. (Information is to the obsessed what clay is to potters.) Fully cognizant of his own ridiculous position, Artaud threw himself at the Great Man's feet. And this was very clever: because while seeming to be "abject," Artaud was actually *using* his abjection to elicit Rivière's tired and pro forma judgments. (Obsessives are a frugal bunch. They find a use for *everything*.) In doing this, Artaud defined Rivière's bland correspondence as a paradigm of the bureaucratic-speak of his country's cultural elite. (Obsession is the need to know some-thing definitively. Does he love me? Artaud was certainly obsessive; and luckily, since he was not a girl, this obsession has been heralded as brilliance. If you're a girl, obsession will much more likely be con-strued as an embarrassing, self-obsessed exposure of your pathetic-ness. Why things work this way is another one of my obsessions. . . .)

Nothing exists without a source. It is important to contextual-ize everything. Needing to understand something, Artaud turned Rivière's witless letters into a dialogue about the very nature of rejection.

Dear James, letters are a talking cure. By writing letters, you learn how to talk, because they are addressed to *someone.*

I started writing to Dick because I'd spent my life being around lots of smart people who thought I was dumb. I was about to turn forty. I had lots of ideas; I just needed someone to talk to. The need to talk is the essence of romantic love, and also of writing. You are alone, you need to feel like someone is listening. At that time I'd spent more than a decade making strange underground movies that nobody wanted. Because then, I was believing in art—which meant, in a very high sense, becoming invisible. I thought art was like a fifth-grade science experiment, or like alchemy—a sort of container where things that you already knew could combust and become something marvelous, didn't.

Making these films was much more obsessive than the simple fact of writing Dick two hundred letters. (See how easy it is?) Making films costs a lot of money, which I didn't have, and I remember coming off a twelve-hour word-processing shift and lining up at the lab with $200 to pick up the five 3-minute Super 8 reels that I fervently believed held the answers to everything. Movies are completely mystical, but no one was listening.

What I discovered, writing to Dick, was I'd missed out on the whole part of art that had to do with authority. People don't know what to think unless someone else tells them. Why did Dick have so much authority? Why didn't I have any? I decided not to give up. I would continue seeing my life as some kind of science experiment, except now I would be absolutely, utterly explicit.

To want to know something, and to be completely direct.

John Cage says: If you do something for five minutes and find that it's boring, try doing it longer.

And Fanny Howe writes: "The truly mad are not content to merely tell stories. They have to act them out."

Dear James, obsession is good. Don't try to have too balanced a life. Seek facts. Human speech is driven, always, by the desire to achieve a goal. Realize you are constantly being manipulated. Remember what's being said is totally defined by who is talking. Learn to enjoy it.

     Love,
     Chris

Katharine Hepburn
Actress

Work as hard as you can, whatever you do, and try to spread generosity of *spirit*.

Rally, rally, rally fascinating.
Katharine Hepburn by Cecil Beaton.
Cecil Beaton photo courtesy of Sotheby's London

Contributors' Notes

MAXX AARDMAN, a writer's writer, is the *nom de plume* of no known Noh gnome. Rather, he is an inkling of his full-size Occidental paterfamilia's desire to realize the truth of the legend that "The Last shall be First." Meanwhile, under the name of his progenitor, MAXX AARDMAN from time to time has been suspected of being, among other things, a major poet of his generation; accordingly, while he has been nominated relentlessly for the Pulitzer prize, he's still holding out for a MacAuthor. Do keep an eye out for *The Maxx Factor* (but once you've bought it, replace that orb before attempting to read or you'll miss half the fun).

JONATHAN AMES is the author of *I Pass Like Night, The Extra Man,* and *What's Not to Love?* His next book, *I'm Not Who You Think I Am,* will be published in May 2002.

LYNDA BARRY, an artist, novelist, and playwright, is the author of numerous books, including *Cruddy: An Illustrated Novel* (Simon & Schuster) and *The! Greatest! Of! Marlys!* (Sasquatch Books).

CHARLES BAXTER is the author (most recently) of a novel, *The Feast of Love* (Vintage) that was a finalist for the National Book Award. He has published two other novels, *First Light* and *Shadow Play,* and four books of stories, most recently *Believers.* He has also published essays on fiction collected in *Burning Down the House,* and has edited or coedited two books of essays, *The Business of Memory* (Graywolf) and *Bringing the Devil to His Knees* (The University of Michigan Press). He has received the Award in Literature from the American Academy of Arts and Letters. He graduated from Macalester College and now lives in Ann Arbor, Michigan, and is adjunct Professor of English at the University of Michigan.

JennIFer BeLLe's first novel, *Going Down,* was named best debut novel of 1996 by *Entertainment Weekly,* translated into many languages, and optioned for the screen, first by Madonna (for whom she wrote the screenplay) and then by Muse Films. Her best-selling second novel, *High Maintenance,* was published in May 2001. Her essays and short stories have appeared in *The New York Times Magazine, Ms.,* the *London Independent Magazine, Mudfish,* and several anthologies. She lives in New York City, where she leads an ongoing writing workshop.

Bruce Benderson is the author of two books of fiction about old Times Square: *Pretending to Say No* (Plume, 1990) and *User* (Dutton, 1994). His manifesto about the decline of urban bohemia, *Toward the New Degeneracy* (Edgewise Press, 1999), was featured in *Rolling Stone.* His new essay, "Sex et solitude," about the death of the city as a place of physical encounters, was published in French by Payot-Rivages in 1999. He is the author of *James Bidgood* (Taschen, 1999), about the author of *Pink Narcissus.* He has written on squatters for *The New York Times,* boxing for *The Village Voice,* unusual shelters for *Nest,* and books and personalities for other publications. He is now completing an erotic-noir memoir about four months of adventures in Romania.

Philosopher, poet, and visionary Hakim Bey, "the Marco Polo of the Subunderground" has been described as a "zealot for the new ideas and concepts necessary for the birth of our intellectual new age." The author of hundreds of articles, most of which can be found on the Internet, his books include *T.A.Z. the Temporary Autonomous Zone, Ontological Anarchy, Poetic Terrorism, Immediatism,* and *Millennium.*

Murray Bookchin has authored more than a dozen books on urbanism, philosophy, ecology, and technology. He is professor emeritus at the School of Environmental Studies, Ramapo College, and director emeritus of the Institute for Social Ecology.

One of the founding members of the beat movement, the "literary outlaw" William S. Burroughs (1914–1997) was the author of many books, including the classic *Naked Lunch, The Soft Machine, The Ticket That Exploded, Nova Express,* and *The Wild Boys.*

JUDITH BUTLER is Maxine Elliot Professor in the departments of Rhetoric and Comparative Literature at the University of California, Berkeley. She is the author of *Subjects of Desire: Hegelian Reflections in Twentieth-Century France* (Columbia University Press, 1987), *Gender Trouble: Feminism and the Subversion of Identity* (Routledge, 1990), *Bodies That Matter: On the Discursive Limits of "Sex"* (Routledge, 1993), *The Psychic Life of Power: Theories in Subjection* (Stanford University Press, 1997), and *Excitable Speech* (Routledge, 1997), as well as numerous articles and contributions on philosophy and feminist and queer theory. Her most recent work on Antigone and the politics of kinship is entitled *Antigone's Claim: Kinship Between Life and Death* (Columbia University Press, 2000). Her new project is a critique of ethical violence that works with modernist philosophical and literary texts.

CAROLYN CHUTE is the author of *The Beans of Egypt, Maine, Letourneau's Used Auto Parts, Merry Men,* and *Snow Man.* She lives in Maine.

ROBERT CREELEY has published more than sixty books of poetry. Born in Arlington, Massachusetts, in 1926, he attended Harvard University but dropped out before taking his degree. His most recent books include *Life & Death* (1998), *Echoes* (1994), and *Selected Poems 1945–1990* (1991). He served as New York State poet laureate from 1989 to 1991 and since 1989 has been Samuel P. Capen Professor of Poetry and Humanities at the State University of New York, Buffalo.

QUENTIN CRISP (1908–1999) is the author of the classic and flamboyantly eccentric coming-of-age memoir *The Naked Civil Servant,* the award-winning film version of which made him an instant international celebrity. Crisp also wrote numerous books and articles about his life and opinions on style, fashion, and the movies. Often hailed as the twentieth-century Oscar Wilde, Crisp was famous for his aphoristic witticisms. He performed his one-man show, *An Evening with Quentin Crisp*, to acclaim in theaters around the world. During part of the show, Crisp answered questions from the audience and gave advice to audience members about how to find their own individual styles and live happy lives. For more information, visit the official Quentin Crisp website, Quentin Crisp Archives, at www.crisperanto.org. (Permission to quote Quentin Crisp's letter to James Harmon granted by the Estate of Quentin Crisp, c/o Clausen, Mays & Tahan Literary Agency. All rights reserved.)

JOE DALLESANDRO (b. 1948) was plucked from the streets of New York City by Andy Warhol and Paul Morrissey in late 1967 and became their male "superstar" in such films as *Lonesome Cowboys, Flesh, Trash,* and *Heat.* His natural charm and often unclothed body made him a sensation of the underground film circuit and eventually a cult figure. His work in Europe includes roles in Paul Morrissey's *Flesh for Frankenstein* and *Blood for Dracula,* Louis Malle's *Black Moon,* Serge Gainsbourg's *Je T'Aime, Moi Non Plus,* and Walerian Borowczyk's *La Marge.* Back in the States, he appeared in Francis Ford Coppola's *The Cotton Club,* John Waters's *Cry-Baby,* and Steven Soderbergh's *The Limey.* He is the subject of an authorized bio-filmography, *Little Joe, Superstar: The Films of Joe Dallesandro,* by Michael Ferguson, and has an official website at www.joedallesandro.com.

RAM DASS has helped raise the consciousness of generations. He is the author of the two-million-copy best-seller *Be Here Now* and most recently published *Still Here.* For more information about Ram Dass's books, tapes, and teaching schedules, go to www.RamDassTapes.org.

"The First Lady of the American Screen," BETTE DAVIS (1908–1989) was considered one of the greatest actresses of the 20th Century. In a career spanning sixty years, she appeared in more than a hundred films, won two Best Actress Academy Awards, and was nominated eight additional times. Feisty, intense, and driven, she took her own advice. For more information, visit www.bettiedavis.com. *(Copyright 2001 Estate of Bette Davis c/o CMG Worldwide. Reprinted with permission.)*

ALAIN DE BOTTON was born in Zurich, Switzerland in 1969. He has written five books, including the novels *Essays in Love* (entitled *On Love* in the U.S.), *The Romantic Movement*, and *Kiss & Tell*. His first nonfiction book, *How Proust Can Change Your Life* was a bestseller in the U.S. and U.K. His next book, an essay on travel, will be published in spring 2002.

MARK DERY ‹markdery@mindspring.com› is a cultural critic. He edited *Flame Wars: The Discourse of Cyberculture* (Duke University Press, 1995) and wrote *Escape Velocity: Cyberculture at the End of the Century* (Grove Press, 1996) [http://www.levity.com]. His collection of essays, *The Pyrotechnic Insanitarium: American Culture on the Brink*, was published by Grove Press in February, 1999. His byline has appeared in *Red Herring, Wired, The New York Times Magazine, Rolling Stone, The Village Voice, Lingua Franca, Suck, Feed,* and *Salon*. His commentaries can be heard nationwide on *Radio Nation*, and he is a frequent lecturer in the U.S. and Europe on new media, fringe thought, and unpopular culture. He is an Assistant Professor in the Department of Journalism and Mass Communications at NYU.

RITA DOVE served as poet laureate of the United States from 1993 to 1995. She has published plays and short stories and several poetry collections, including *Thomas and Beulah*, which won the Pulitzer prize in 1987, and *On the Bus with Rosa Parks* (1999). She is Commonwealth Professor of English at the University of Virginia in Charlottesville.

MICHAEL THOMAS FORD is the author of numerous books, including the essay collections *Alec Baldwin Doesn't Love Me, That's Mr. Faggot to You, It's Not Mean If It's True,* and *The Little Book of Neuroses*. If you really want to know more, you can visit him at www.michaelthomasford.com.

MARY GAITSKILL is the author of the short story collections *Bad Behavior* and *Because They Wanted To,* as well as the novel *Two Girls, Fat and Thin*. Her work has been translated into twelve foreign languages; *Because They Wanted To* was nominated for the Pen/Faulkner award in 1998. She greatly admires James Harmon's perseverance in this project, and if she had a piece of advice to give, particularly to young writers, she would suggest that they be as perseverant.

MARTHA GELLHORN (1908–1998) was one of the great war correspondents of the twentieth century. In a career that spanned nearly fifty years, she covered everything from the Spanish Civil War to the U.S. invasion of Panama. Besides her journalism, she authored seven novels and four collections of short stories. Smart, sexy, and beautiful, she was married to Ernest Hemingway from 1940 to 1946. She was the only one of his wives to leave him.

SPALDING GRAY is a writer, actor, and performer. He is the author of *Swimming to Cambodia, Monster in a Box, It's a Slippery Slope,* and *Morning, Noon, and Night.* He lives with his family in New York.

JIM HARRISON is the author of seven collections of poetry, a collection of nonfiction, *Just Before Dark,* and many novels and novellas, including *Legends of the Fall, The Woman Lit by Fireflies, Julip, The Road Home, Sundog, Dalva,* and others. His most recent book is *The Beast God Forgot to Invent.*

MARK HELPRIN is the award winning author of *A Dove of the East and Other Stories, A Soldier of the Great War, Winter's Tale, Ellis Island and Other Stories,* and *Memoir from Antproof Case.*

Known for her independent spirit, the fiercely talented actress KATHARINE HEPBURN consistently makes the lists of the world's most admired women. In a career spanning six decades, she is the only woman to win four Academy Awards as best actress. She is the author of *Me: Stories of My Life* and *The Making of the African Queen, or, How I Went to Africa with Bogart, Bacall, and Huston and Almost Lost My Mind.* She lives in Connecticut.

A self-proclaimed "Jewish Road Warrior," ABBIE HOFFMAN (1936–1989) was the preeminent U.S. political radical of the '60s, '70s, and '80s and epitomized youth peace activism and community organizing. His books include *Revolution for the Hell of It*, *Woodstock Nation*, *Steal This Book*, *The Autobiography of Abbie Hoffman*, *Square Dancing in the Ice Age: Underground Writings*, and *Steal This Urine Test*. His archives are with the Abbie Hoffman Activist Foundation, Inc.

STEWART HOME is to literature what slapstick is to comedy. Home is the author of more than a dozen works of fiction and cultural commentary, including *Confusion Incorporated: A Collection of Lies, Hoaxes & Hidden Truths*, *Come Before Christ and Murder Love*, *Blow Job*, *Slow Death*, and forthcoming in spring 2002, *69 Things to Do with a Dead Princess*. Home is a nomad who divides his time between drinking Adnams Suffolk ales and Islay single malts. Geographically, Home is most usually to be found in northwest Europe, but insists that because America is a concept rather than a geographical location, he has always dwelt in the USA. Just like his spiritual father, Sun Ra, Home actually comes from the planet Saturn.

HORST P. HORST (1906–1999) was considered a master of twentieth-century photography. His subjects included icons of stage, screen, and the arts: Katharine Hepburn, Coco Chanel, Noël Coward, Salvador Dalí, Bette Davis, W. H. Auden, etc. His lush, elegant photographs are featured in *Horst Portraits: 60 Years of Style* (Abrams, 2001).

Columnist, reporter, novelist, DAN JENKINS is the author of numerous works of fiction and nonfiction, including *Semi-Tough*, *Rude Behavior*, *Dead Solid Perfect*, and *The Money-Whipped Steer-Job Three-Jack Give-Up Artist: A Novel*. He lives in Texas.

KEN KESEY (1935–2001) was the author of *One Flew Over the Cuckoo's Nest*, *Sometimes a Great Notion*, and *Sailor Song*. He lived in Oregon.

FLORENCE KING is the author of nine books, including the best-selling *Confessions of a Failed Southern Lady* and *Southern Ladies and Gentlemen*. She is currently a columnist for the *National Review*.

wayne koestenbaum is the author of five books of prose: *Double Talk* (1989), *The Queen's Throat* (1993), *Jackie Under My Skin* (1995), *Cleavage* (2000), and *Andy Warhol* (2001). He is the author of three books of poetry: *Ode to Anna Moffo and Other Poems* (1990), *Rhapsodies of a Repeat Offender* (1994), and *The Milk of Inquiry* (2001). He is professor of English at the Graduate Center of the City University of New York.

paul krassner, "the father of the underground press," is an award-winning satirist, writer, and stand-up comedian. Publisher of *The Realist,* the satirical magazine for adults, his autobiography, *Confessions of a Raving, Unconfined Nut: Misadventures in the Counter-Culture,* was published by Simon & Schuster in 1994. His other books include *The Winner of the Slow Bicycle Race: The Satirical Writings of Paul Krassner* and *Sex, Drugs, and the Twinkie Murders.* He lives in Venice, California.

chris kraus is the founder/editor of Semiotext(e)'s Native Agents new fiction series. A filmmaker and teacher, she is the author of *I Love Dick* and *Aliens & Anorexia.* Her latest book, edited with her husband, Sylvere Lotringer, is *Hatred of Capitalism: A Semiotext(e) Reader* (2001).

bruce labruce is a Toronto-based filmmaker, writer, and photographer. He began his career in the mid-1980s making a series of short experimental Super 8 films and coediting a punk fanzine called *J.D.s,* which begat the queercore movement. He has directed and starred in three feature-length movies, *No Skin Off My Ass* (1991), *Super 8½* (1994), and *Hustler White* (1996). He also wrote the premature memoir *The Reluctant Pornographer,* published by Gutter Press, which will be followed by a sequel, *Porno for Dummies,* in 2002. A book on LaBruce's work, *Ride, Queer, Ride,* was published in 1998 by the Plug-In Gallery in Winnipeg, Canada. LaBruce is a contributing editor and frequent writer and photographer for *Index* magazine and a regular columnist for *Eye Weekly* and *Exclaim* magazines, as well as the U.S. porno mags *Honcho* and *Playguy.*

ALPHONSO LINGIS is a professor of philosophy at Penn State University. His books include *Excesses: Eros and Culture* (1984), *Libido: The French Existential Theories* (1985), *Phenomenological Explanations* (1986), *Deathbound Subjectivity* (1989), *The Community of Those Who Have Nothing in Common* (1994), *Abuses* (1994), *Foreign Bodies* (1994), *Sensation: Intelligibility in Sensibility* (1995), *The Imperative* (1998), and *Dangerous Emotions* (2000).

BRET LOTT is the author of five novels, two story collections, and a memoir. He lives in Mt. Pleasant, South Carolina, with his wife and two sons, and is a writer-in-residence at the College of Charleston. He also directs the MFA program at Vermont College.

LYDIA LUNCH is a confrontationalist who works in many mediums. For more information go to www.lydialunch.org.

VALERIE MARTIN is the author of *Salvation: Scenes from the Life of St. Francis*. She has also written two collections of short fiction and six novels, including *Italian Fever, The Great Divorce,* and *Mary Reilly.* She lives in upstate New York.

Born in Seattle, MARY MCCARTHY (1912–1989) was the author of twenty-eight books of fiction and nonfiction. Known for her sophisticated and biting wit, she is considered one of America's preeminent twentieth-century literary figures. Her autobiographical novels include *Memories of a Catholic Girlhood* and *The Group. (Courtesy of the Mary McCarthy trust)*

RICHARD MELTZER's first book, *The Aesthetics of Rock,* published in 1970, is considered a classic of rock criticism. The author of a dozen books, he has also written for *The Village Voice,* the *L.A. Reader,* the *L.A. Weekly, Spin, Rolling Stone,* and others. He is the vocalist for the band Smegma and lives in Portland, Oregon.

A pioneer in the philosophy of sex, Dr. JOHN MONEY has been called the "foremost theoretician of human sexual relations in the twentieth century." He is the author of *Venuses Penuses; The Adam Principle; Sin, Science, and the Sex Police;* and *Love Maps.* He is professor emeritus of medical psychology and pediatrics at Johns Hopkins University.

EILEEN MYLES is considered one of the most popular poets in America today. Author of *Not Me* and *Chelsea Girls,* her most recent book is *Cool for You.* She lives in New York.

ARTHUR NERSESIAN was born and raised in New York City. He is the author of four novels. His latest book is *Suicide Casanova,* published by Akashic Books.

LARRY NIVEN is the Nebula Award–winning author of such classics as *Ringworld, The Integral Trees, Tales of Known Space,* and *Dream Park.* He also created the popular Man-Kzin Wars series and is the coauthor of *The Mote in God's Eye, Lucifer's Hammer, Beowulf's Children,* and the *New York Times* bestseller *Footfall.* He lives in Tarzana, California.

MARTHA C. NUSSBAUM is Ernst Freund Distinguished Service Professor of Law and Ethics at the University of Chicago, with appointments in the Law School, Philosophy Department, and Divinity School. She is an associate in Classics, an affiliate of the Committee for Southern Asian Studies, and a member of the board of the Center for Gender Studies. In 2000 she was president of the American Philosophical Association's Central Division. Her recent books include *Sex and Social Justice* (1999), *Women and Human Development* (2002), and *Upheavals of Thought: The Intelligence of Emotions* (2000).

ANITA O'DAY, "The Jezebel of Jazz," was born Anita Belle Colton in 1919. She's considered one of the greatest jazz vocalists of our time. Check her out at www.anitaoday.com.

A living legend, the '50s model BETTIE PAGE is considered one of the greatest pin-ups of all time. With her signature cropped bangs, voluptuous figure, and infectious smile, the raven-haired beauty's influence can still be seen today in art, fashion, film, and magazines. A true pop-culture icon, her official website is www.bettiepage.com.

CAMILLE PAGLIA, the scholar and culture critic, is university professor and professor of humanities and media studies at the University of the Arts in Philadelphia, where she has taught since 1984. She received her B.A. from the State University of New York at Binghamton in 1968 and her M.Phil. and Ph.D. degrees from Yale University in 1971 and 1974, respectively. She is a bestselling author who has written four books: *Sexual Personae: Art and Decadence from Nefertiti to Emily Dickinson* (Yale University Press, 1990), *Sex, Art, and American Culture: Essays* (Vintage Books, 1992), *Vamps & Tramps: New Essays* (Vintage Books, 1994), and *The Birds,* a study of Alfred Hitchcock published in 1998 by the British Film Institute in its Film Classics series. Her work has been widely translated abroad. Professor Paglia has contributed innumerable articles on art, literature, popular culture, feminism, and politics to publications around the world, including Salon.com, for which she has written a regular column. She has lectured and appeared on television and radio extensively in the United States and abroad. She is currently completing a study of poetry for Pantheon Books, as well as assembling her third essay collection for Vintage Books.

C. D. PAYNE is the author of the comic novel *Youth in Revolt: The Journals of Nick Twisp* and its sequel *Revolting Youth: The Further Journals of Nick Twisp.* His other works include *Civic Beauties, Frisco Pigeon Mambo, Queen of America,* and *Cut to the Twisp.* Widely published in Europe, he is unaccountably famous in the Czech Republic.

RICHARD POWERS is an award-winning novelist whose books include *Three Farmers on Their Way to a Dance, Prisoner's Dilemma, Operation Wandering Soul, The Gold Bug Variations, Galatea 2.2, Gain,* and *Plowing the Dark.* He is currently working on a novel about time, music, and race. He teaches at the University of Illinois at Urbana-Champaign.

One of the twentieth century's greatest thinkers, the philosopher WILLArD van orman Quine was recognized as a world leader in set theory, mathematical logic, and the philosophy of language. He died Christmas Day 2000.

JOHn RECHY is the first novelist to receive PEN-USA-West's Life-time Achievement Award; he is also the recipient of the Publishing Triangle's William Whitehead Achievement Award. He is the author of thirteen novels, including *City of Night, Bodies and Souls,* and *The Coming of the Night.* His work has been translated into more than a dozen languages.

Novelist TOM ROBBINS is the author of numerous books, including *Another Roadside Attraction, Jitterbug Perfume, Even Cowgirls Get the Blues, Skinny Legs and All,* and *Fierce Invalids Home from Hot Climates.* He lives in Washington.

SCOTT RUSSELL Sanders has won the Lannan Literary Award and the Great Lakes Book Award. His books include *Hunting for Hope, The Paradise of Bombs, Secrets of the Universe,* and *The Force of Spirit.* He teaches at Indiana University and lives in Bloomington.

GEORGE Saunders is the author of two short story collections, *CivilWarLand in Bad Decline* and *Pastoralia,* and the children's book *The Very Persistent Gappers of Frip,* illustrated by Lane Smith. He teaches in the creative writing program at Syracuse University and was recently listed by *The New Yorker* as one of the twenty best American writers forty and under.

Dr. Laura Schlessinger is an internationally syndicated radio talk-show host and is the author of *The Ten Commandments, How Could You Do That?!, Ten Stupid Things Women Do to Mess Up Their Lives, Ten Stupid Things Men Do to Mess Up Their Lives, Parenthood by Proxy* (paperback: *Stupid Things Parents Do to Mess Up Their Kids*), *Ten Stupid Things Couples Do to Mess Up Their Relationships,* and the children's books *Why Do You Love Me?*, *But I Waaannt It!*, and *Growing Up Is Hard.*

JOANNA SCOTT is the author of five novels, including *Arrogance, The Manikin,* and *Make Believe,* and a collection of stories, *Various Antidotes.* She teaches at the University of Rochester.

Philosopher, writer, publisher, editor, composer, journalist, broadcaster, and businessman ROGER SCRUTON is the author of more than twenty books, including *An Intelligent Person's Guide to Philosophy* (1996) and *An Intelligent Person's Guide to Modern Culture.* He lives in England.

BOB SHACOCHIS's first book of short stories, *Easy in the Islands,* won the National Book Award. His works of fiction and non-fiction include *The Next New World, Swimming in the Volcano, Domesticity,* and *The Immaculate Invasion.* His journalism and essays appear frequently in *Harper's* and other national magazines. He lives in Florida and New Mexico.

LUCIUS SHEPARD won the Nebula award for his novella "R&R" and has won the World Fantasy Award for both *The Jaguar Hunter* and *The Ends of the Earth.* He also won the Hugo award for his novella "Barnacle Bill the Spacer." His novels include *Green Eyes, Life During Wartime,* and *The Golden.* He lives in California.

CINDY SHERMAN is one of the leading artists of our time. She lives in New York City.

JOHN SHIRLEY is the winner of the Bram Stoker Award for his story collection *Black Butterflies: A Flock on the Dark Side,* and is the author of numerous novels, including the forthcoming *Demons* from Ballantine/Del Rey and *And the Angel with Television Eyes* from Night

Shade books. He's also the author of the nonfiction book *Gurdjieff: A Sketch of His Life and Ideas,* coming from Lindisfarne Press. He writes television and film scripts from time to time also. The authorized fan-created website is www.darkecho.com/johnshirley.

Ian Shoales is the nom de fume of writer and performer Merle Kessler. He lives in San Francisco. A collection of Ian Shoales' commentary, *Not Wet Yet,* is available from 2.13.61 Press. Go to www.two1361.com.

Mark Simpson was born in York, England, in 1965. After leaving school he tried his hand at a number of exciting professions including doorman, deckhand, laborer, sperm donor, nude male model, pot-washer, and double-glazing salesman before he realized he was terminally unemployable and so turned to writing. His books include *Male Impersonators, It's a Queer World, Anti-Gay,* and *The Queen Is Dead.* He has been variously described by the press as "a queer captain Kirk," "a brainy thug," "brilliantly buccaneering," "a skinhead Oscar Wilde," "Joe Don Baker channeling Truman Capote," and "a cunt." His new book, *Sex Terror,* is published by the Haworth Press. For more info, go to www.marksimpson.com.

R. U. Sirius is one of the icons of cyberculture. He is best known as the editor-in-chief of *MONDO 2000,* the technoculture magazine of the early '90s. His most recent book is *The Revolution: Quotations from Revolution Party Chairman R. U. Sirius.*

Steve Stern is the award-winning author of several works of fiction, including *A Plague of Dreamers* and *The Wedding Jester.* He lives and teaches in Saratoga Springs, New York.

Richard Taylor is an American analytic philosopher. His works include *Action and Purpose, Good and Evil,* and the classic, *Metaphysics.*

ALEXANDER THEROUX has taught at Harvard, Yale, MIT, and the University of Virginia. He is the author of numerous books of fiction and nonfiction, including *Three Wogs, Darconville's Cat, An Adultery, The Primary Colors,* and *The Lollipop Trollops and Other Poems.* He lives in West Barnstable, Massachusetts.

MAURICE VELLEKOOP is an artist and illustrator. His books include *Vellevision, Maurice Vellekoop's ABC Book,* and the series *Men's Room.* His work can be seen in various magazines and anthologies. He lives in Canada.

VERUSCHKA (a.k.a. Countess Vera von Lehndorff) is the legendary supermodel. Known for her unconventional beauty, she is an actress, artist, and filmmaker. She lives and works in New York City.

WILLIAM T. VOLLMANN is the author of *An Afghanistan Picture Show, You Bright and Risen Angels, The Rainbow Stories, Whores for Gloria, Thirteen Stories and Thirteen Epitaphs, Butterfly Stories, The Atlas,* and *The Royal Family.* His latest book is *Argall,* the fourth volume of his "Seven Dreams" series, which includes *The Ice-Shirt, Fathers and Crows,* and *The Rifles.* He resides in California.

DIANE WAKOWSKI has published more than twenty collections of poetry, her most recent being new and selected poems, *The Butcher's Apron,* from Black Sparrow Press. In 1989 her selected poems, *Emerald Ice,* won the William Carlos Williams Prize from the Poetry Society of America. She is Poet-in-Residence at Michigan State University.

In addition to plays and nonfiction, novelist **FAY WELDON** is the author of *Big Girls Don't Cry, Wicked Women, Splitting, The Life and Loves of a She-Devil, Rhode Island Blues,* and most recently, *The Bulgari Connection.*

One of America's major artists, the controversial JOEL-PETER WITKIN has won numerous awards and his highly sought-after work has been exhibited worldwide. He lives in New Mexico.

GENE WOLFE is the winner of the World Fantasy Award for Lifetime Achievement, the Nebula Award, the World Fantasy Award, the John W. Campbell Memorial Award, the British Fantasy Award, and the Prix Apollo. He lives in Illinois.

JOHN ZERZAN is the author of *Elements of Refusal* and *Future Primitive*. He coedited, with Alice Carnes, *Questioning Technology,* and edited *Against Civilization*. He has written numerous articles, many of which can be found on the web, and is working on a new collection of essays. He lives in Eugene, Oregon.

HOWARD ZINN, in his own words a "historical engineer," is best known for his best-selling book, *A People's History of the United States*. He is professor emeritus of political science at Boston University.